Cooking in Everyday ENGLISH

THE ABCs OF GREAT FLAVOR AT HOME

by TODD ENGLISH

with Amanda Haas

Oxmoor House®

ISBN-13: 978-0-8487-3484-8
ISBN-10: 0-8487-3484-X
Library of Congress Control Number: 2011931386

Printed in the United States of America
First Printing 2011

Oxmoor House
VP, Publishing Director: Jim Childs
Editorial Director: Susan Payne Dobbs
Brand Manager: Vanessa Tiongson
Senior Editor: Rebecca Brennan
Managing Editor: Laurie S. Herr

Cooking in Everyday English
Editor: Katherine Cobbs
Project Editor: Holly D. Smith
Senior Designer: Melissa M. Clark
Director, Test Kitchens: Elizabeth Tyler Austin
Assistant Directors, Test Kitchens: Julie Christopher, Julie Gunter
Test Kitchens Professionals: Wendy Ball, Allison E. Cox, Victoria E. Cox,
    Margaret Monroe Dickey, Alyson Moreland Haynes, Stefanie Maloney,
    Callie Nash, Catherine Crowell Steele, Leah Van Deren
Photography Director: Jim Bathie
Senior Photo Stylist: Kay E. Clarke
Associate Photo Stylist: Katherine Eckert Coyne
Assistant Photo Stylist: Mary Louise Menendez
Production Manager: Theresa Beste-Farley

Contributors
Writer: Amanda Haas
Recipe Editor: Ashley Leath
Copy Editors: Jacqueline Giovanelli, Dolores Hydock
Proofreaders: Rebecca Benton, Norma McKittrick
Indexer: Nanette Cardon
Interns: Erin Bishop, Sarah H. Doss, Blair Gillespie, Alison Loughman,
    Caitlin Watzke
Photographer: Mary Britton Senseney, Jason Wallis

Time Home Entertainment Inc.
Publisher: Richard Fraiman
VP, Strategy & Business Development: Steven Sandonato
Executive Director, Marketing Services: Carol Pittard
Executive Director, Retail & Special Sales: Tom Mifsud
Executive Director, New Product Development: Peter Harper
Director, Bookazine Development & Marketing: Laura Adam
Publishing Director: Joy Butts
Finance Director: Glenn Buonocore
Associate General Counsel: Helen Wan

To order additional publications, call 1-800-765-6400 or 1-800-491-0551.

For more books to enrich your life, visit **oxmoorhouse.com**
To search, savor, and share thousands of recipes, visit **myrecipes.com**

Cover: Roasted Beet Salad with Goat Cheese and Pistachios (page 79), Ginger-Soy Skirt Steak (page 212), and Corn Raita (page 29)
Front flap: Oven-Roasted Brussels Sprouts with Apples, Onions, and Crispy Bacon (page 110)

Editor's Note: Consuming raw or undercooked meats, poultry, seafood, shellfish, or eggs may increase your risk of foodborne illness. If you are concerned about these health risks, avoid eating raw eggs, and cook meats, poultry, seafood, or shellfish to appropriate doneness.

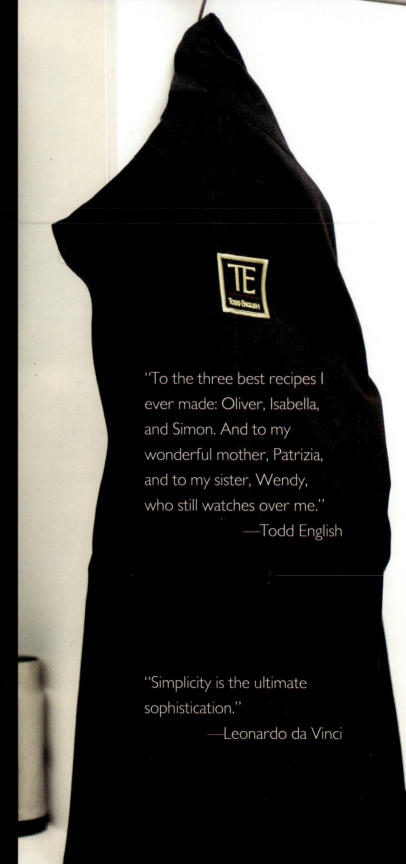

"To the three best recipes I ever made: Oliver, Isabella, and Simon. And to my wonderful mother, Patrizia, and to my sister, Wendy, who still watches over me."

—Todd English

"Simplicity is the ultimate sophistication."

—Leonardo da Vinci

contents

6

Introduction

"I LOVE TO COOK. Cooking has never been a chore, but a passion in my life. Though it's my chosen work, I've always kept it in perspective. It's not rocket science after all. Cooking is a way to connect with others while enjoying one of life's daily pleasures—food!

For me, there is no greater pleasure than cooking at home, surrounded by my friends and family. It's a way to show my love for those I care about most and one of the few chances I have to connect with others minus interruptions from the outside world. Creating this cookbook has been a wonderful way to enjoy extra time with them. Each recipe was created in my own kitchen and critiqued by my most vocal critics—my friends and family. (My three children have developed very strong opinions about food!) That collective input has filled this book with some of our favorite dishes, and it's a true reflection of how I cook at home.

I hope to get you thinking about food and combinations of flavors in a new way, so you come to understand why certain ingredients complement one another and tantalize the palate. With my help, you will become fearless in the kitchen! I also hope you'll gain appreciation of food beyond simple nourishment and begin to look at it as an avenue to feed the soul and strengthen communal bonds. I promise *Cooking in Everyday English* approaches cooking in a whole new way!"

Todd English

Basics

We all need a place to start in the kitchen, so I've put my favorite building blocks together for you here. Spice blends, sauces, doughs, vinaigrettes, and fresh pastas are great recipes to master because you will use them again and again to create amazing meals. This chapter is a reflection of the direction my kitchen has taken—away from the heavier hand of preparations of the past—to focus instead on whole spices, herbs, and the ingredients themselves, allowing their intrinsic flavors to shine. Once you ace the recipes in this chapter, you'll be on your way to becoming a phenomenal cook.

Todd's Pantry

A well-stocked pantry equals delicious possibilities at mealtime. The list below includes the ingredients I always keep on hand.

Pantry

Dried Spices

Aleppo pepper, ground
Allspice, whole and ground
Ancho chile powder
Bay leaves
Cardamom pods, whole or ground
Cayenne
Cinnamon, sticks and ground
Coriander seeds, whole or ground
Crushed red pepper
Cumin seeds, whole or ground
Curry powder
Fennel seeds, whole
Ginger, ground
Marjoram
Nutmeg, whole or ground
Oregano
Paprika, Hungarian and smoked
Peppercorns, black and green
Red pepper flakes, crushed
Saffron threads
Sesame seeds, toasted; black and white
Sumac, ground
Thyme
Turmeric
Vanilla beans, Tahitian
Vanilla extract

Dry Goods

Anchovy fillets, canned both in oil and in salt
Artichoke hearts and bottoms, canned
Baking chocolate (Callebaut or El Rey), bittersweet
Baking powder
Baking soda
Balsamic vinegar, white
Brown sugar, dark and light
Canola oil
Caraway seeds
Chickpeas, canned and dried
Chocolate, semisweet
Chocolate, unsweetened
Chocolate, white
Cloves, whole
Cocoa powder (Callebaut or Droste), unsweetened
Cornmeal, stone-ground yellow
Cornstarch
Fish sauce
Flour, assorted
Garlic, granulated
Hoisin sauce
Honey
Lentils, assorted
Mustard, assorted
Oats, rolled
Olive oil, virgin and extra virgin

Panko breadcrumbs
Pasta, assorted shapes
Powdered sugar
Rice, assorted
Salt, kosher; coarse and fine sea
San Marzano tomatoes, canned whole and canned crushed
Semolina flour
Sesame oil, dark and toasted
Sesame tahini, canned
Soy sauce or tamari
Sriracha sauce
Tomato paste
Vegetable oil
Vietnamese chile paste
Vinegar, cider, light and dark balsamic, red wine, rice, sherry, white
White cannellini beans, dried or canned
White sugar (granulated)
Wine, red, rosé, and white

Refrigerator

Butter, unsalted
Eggs, large
Mayonnaise
Olives, assorted
Parmigiano-Reggiano cheese (in a chunk)
Pecorino Romano cheese (in a chunk)

Freezer

Bacon, slab
Butter, unsalted
Peas
Spinach
Vanilla-bean ice cream

Todd's Kitchen Tools

The right tools make cooking a pleasure. You don't need a lot of fancy gadgets, only those that get the job done well. My favorites are outlined below.

Knives

8-inch chef's
9-inch or 10-inch slicing
Boning
Paring
Santoku or cleaver
Serrated bread

Pots and Pans

8-qt. stockpot
8-inch heavy cast-iron skillet
10-inch heavy skillet
14-inch heavy skillet
Dutch oven
Ridged grill pan
Sauté pans, 7-inch and 10-inch

Electrics

2-qt. electric ice-cream maker
Blender (Vitamix)
Coffee grinder
Food processor

Juicer
Stand mixer

Equipment

Charcoal, hardwood
Cheese grater
Colander
Cutting board, heavy wooden
Food mill
Grill, charcoal or wood-burning
Japanese mandoline
Ladle
Measuring cups
Measuring spoons
Mixing bowls, stainless steel
Mortar and pestle
Potato masher
Sieve
Slotted spoons
Spatulas
Tongs
Vegetable peeler
Whisks
Wooden spoons

Salt

"Knowing how to salt food properly is the difference between being a decent cook and a great one. Poorly salted food takes all the pleasure out of eating. Not enough, and the best ingredients taste lackluster. Too much salt, and your palate is wrecked for the rest of the meal. Salt enhances flavor unlike any other ingredient. Used properly, it elevates the flavor of a simple grilled steak and brings out the chocolate and caramel notes in a cookie.

If you consider yourself a salt junkie, there's only one way I can teach you how to salt food properly: You need a salt detox! Take an entire week off from salt and stick to a diet of fruits, veggies, lean proteins, and grains while drinking a lot of water. Yes, your food will taste a little bland, but your palate will begin to readjust and develop a baseline for how much salt you really need. After that, you can begin to use salt as a complement to ingredients such as spices, herbs, and citrus—not as a cover-up.

As a cook, I believe that unless you're baking, salt should always be used to taste. Throwing salt blindly into a pan as your food cooks is a gamble that's hard to remedy if you've overdone it. I prefer to add a little bit of salt throughout the cooking process to gradually build flavor. At the end of cooking, really taste the food. Adjust the seasoning and taste again. As you practice restraint, you will begin to see how small amounts of salt can highlight a dish just enough to bring out its best. Try this approach, and you will use much less salt than if you throw it in randomly. For most recipes in this book, I provide an exact salt measurement to use as a baseline to help you get started.

Experiment with different types of salt. For everyday cooking, I turn to kosher salt, and it's what I recommend in most of my recipes. Kosher salt isn't too "salty" so you can add some and taste, then add more if you need it. It also dissolves easily into sauces and liquids. I really try to stay away from iodized salt, as it creates a kind of chemical backlash and numbs your tongue. I also love playing with sea salts, sel gris, and even Himalayan salt. A great way to remember how to pair salts with food is to think 'Earth to Earth' and 'Sea to Sea.' Experiment with mineral salts mined from the earth on meat and produce and use sea salts on fish and seafood.

When salting protein, there are two schools of thought: You can salt the protein before cooking it and really rub it in so it is absorbed; or, you can cook the Tuscan way without any salt at all, and use it as a condiment to sprinkle on the food when it's done. Sometimes I'll grill T-bones or rib-eyes without salt, then serve them rare with salt on the side as a condiment. I also typically salt a tuna fillet before I sear it, allowing the tuna to really soak up the briny flavor. There's no right or wrong, just preferences! So play around.

Once you understand what salt does, use it to your advantage. Pick a few of your favorite seeds and spices and begin to mix them with salt. Freshly ground coriander and cumin seeds, cinnamon, and curry powder are a few that can be blended with salt. Fresh herbs and citrus zest also mix beautifully to create flavored salts for sprinkling."

Here are two of my homemade salt combos:

Fennel Salt: Zest a few oranges, and allow the zest to sit on the counter overnight to dry out somewhat. Place 1 Tbsp. fennel seed, 1 tsp. orange zest, and 2 Tbsp. kosher or sea salt in a pepper mill or salt grinder on the finest setting. Then cook a piece of fish or chicken with very little salt and pepper, and grind the fresh salt combination over the top. It's so delicious; it's almost like a sauce.

Rosemary and Lemon Salt: Chop 2 Tbsp. fresh rosemary and zest 2 lemons, leaving it all on the counter to dry out overnight. Place them in a salt grinder, add ½ cup sea salt, and grind over lamb chops, vegetables, and steak.

Vinaigrettes

"While I still love classic sauces like béchamel and hollandaise, lighter, flavorful vinaigrettes are what I turn to most often. Once you master the vinaigrette, you'll find that you can add almost any type of aromatic to change up the flavors; shallots, fresh herbs, spices, and citrus are a few of the things I use in mine. I serve them alongside grilled meats, as a dressing for tabbouleh and fattoush, and even as a marinade. As you start to experiment, remember this rule of thumb: Use one part acid (vinegar, citrus juice, etc.) to three parts oil, and always remember to add salt and pepper."

Basic Vinaigrette

Shallots, 3 Tbsp. minced
Dijon mustard, 2 Tbsp.
Kosher salt, ½ tsp.

Freshly ground black pepper, ¼ tsp.
Sherry vinegar, ½ cup
Extra virgin olive oil, 1 ½ cups

1 Whisk together first 5 ingredients in a medium bowl. Gradually whisk in oil. 2½ cups

Lemon Vinaigrette

Ground sumac, 1 ½ tsp.
Kosher salt, ½ tsp.
Freshly ground black pepper, ¼ tsp.
Ground Aleppo pepper, ⅛ tsp.

Fresh lemon juice, 6 Tbsp.
White balsamic vinegar, 1 ½ tsp.
Extra virgin olive oil, 1 cup

1 Whisk together first 6 ingredients in a medium bowl. Gradually whisk in oil. 1⅓ cups

Orange-Mint Vinaigrette

"Using the zest of citrus infuses a recipe with flavor and aroma without acidity. Orange and mint were made for each other."

Orange zest, 2 Tbsp.

Fresh mint leaves, 2 Tbsp. minced

Fresh orange juice, ¾ cup

White balsamic vinegar, 3 Tbsp.

Honey, 2 tsp.

Extra virgin olive oil, 1 cup

❶ Whisk together first 5 ingredients in a medium bowl. Gradually whisk in oil. 1¼ cups

Harissa Vinaigrette

Za'atar Spice Blend (page 21), 1 tsp.

Sugar, 1 tsp.

Kosher salt, ½ tsp.

Harissa paste, 2 Tbsp.

White vinegar, 1 Tbsp.

Fresh lime juice, 1 tsp.

Extra virgin olive oil, 1 cup

❶ Whisk together first 6 ingredients in a medium bowl. Gradually whisk in oil. 1⅛ cups

Note: To make your own harissa paste, soak 6 small, dried red chile peppers in 1 cup hot water 30 minutes or until softened. Drain, reserving ⅓ cup soaking liquid. Remove stems from peppers (leave the seeds). Process peppers, reserved ⅓ cup soaking liquid, 8 garlic cloves, 1 (2-inch) piece fresh ginger, and 1 tsp. salt in a blender until mixture forms a coarse paste. Add 1 Tbsp. ground cumin and 1 Tbsp. ground coriander. With blender running, add ½ cup olive oil in a slow, steady stream, processing until coarsely blended.

Compound Butters

"It's the little things in the kitchen that can make all the difference. Take 5 minutes to make one of these butters and pop it in the freezer. Then on a busy night you can enhance the flavor of any simple grilled meat, pasta, or vegetable dish."

A.C.G. Butter

"Anchovies, capers, and garlic are the essence of my first restaurant, Olives. I turn to these three ingredients again and again, and encourage you to prepare this yourself so you can see what incredible depth of flavor they add to any recipe. This continues to be my ultimate flavor combination."

Capers, 2 tsp. drained and rinsed
Anchovies, 2 Tbsp.
Extra virgin olive oil, 1 Tbsp.
Garlic, 2 cloves minced

Unsalted butter, 1 cup cold cut up
Kosher salt, ½ tsp.
Freshly ground black pepper, ¼ tsp.

❶ Pat capers dry with a paper towel. Place capers, anchovies, oil, and garlic in a small saucepan. Cook, stirring often, over medium heat 3 minutes or until mixture begins to brown. Remove from heat. Let cool 5 minutes.

❷ Process anchovy mixture, butter, salt, and pepper in a food processor until smooth. Store in an airtight container in the refrigerator. About 1 cup

Note: If desired, chill butter until cool enough to shape into a log. Wrap in heavy-duty plastic wrap and seal in a zip-top plastic freezer bag. Freeze up to 3 months.

Blue Cheese–Almond Butter

"This butter becomes the crust for my Double-Cut Pork Chops (page 180) when melted under the broiler. It is equally delicious in burgers or slathered on crostini."

Slivered almonds, ¾ cup toasted
Unsalted butter, 1 cup softened
Blue cheese, ¾ cup crumbled

Kosher salt, ½ tsp.
Freshly ground black pepper, ½ tsp.
Panko breadcrumbs, 1 cup

❶ Pulse almonds in a food processor 15 times or until consistency of coarse meal. Add butter and next 3 ingredients; process until combined. Add panko; process until combined, stopping to scrape down sides as needed. 2 cups

Rosemary and Garlic Butter

"Stir this classic Italian flavor combination into simple starches like my Master Risotto (page 124) or Semolina Polenta (page 122)."

Garlic, 3 cloves
Unsalted butter, 1 cup cold cut up
Fresh rosemary, 2 Tbsp. chopped
Kosher salt, 1 tsp.
Freshly ground black pepper, ½ tsp.

❶ With processor running, drop garlic through food chute. Process until finely chopped. Add butter and remaining ingredients; process until smooth. Store in an airtight container in the refrigerator up to a few days or freeze for up to 3 months. About 1 cup

Note: If desired, chill butter until cool enough to shape into a log. Wrap in heavy-duty plastic wrap and seal in a zip-top plastic freezer bag. Freeze up to 3 months.

Mint Butter

"Clean. Bright. The perfect accompaniment for pureed peas or roasted carrots. It's great over my Greek Island Lamb Chops (page 175) as well."

Fresh mint leaves, ½ cup loosely packed
Shallot, 1 medium halved
Unsalted butter, 1 cup cold cut up
Kosher salt, 1 tsp.
Freshly ground black pepper, ½ tsp.

❶ Process mint in a food processor until minced. Add shallot; pulse until chopped. Add butter and remaining ingredients; process until smooth. Store in an airtight container in the refrigerator up to 2 days or freeze up to 3 months. About 1 cup

Note: If desired, chill butter until cool enough to shape into a log. Wrap in heavy-duty plastic wrap and seal in a zip-top plastic freezer bag. Freeze up to 3 months.

Spice Blends

"I can't say enough about how a teaspoon of a thoughtful combination of spices can add enchanted flavor to practically any recipe—grilled meats, fish, roasted vegetables, vinaigrettes. The following blends are those I turn to again and again. Store batches in airtight containers in a cool, dark place for up to two months."

Mexican Spice Blend

"I love using this spice blend when I make my Prime Rib Chili (page 174), or even sprinkling it over grilled meats for tacos. It adds a subtle amount of spice to chicken, beef, and fish."

Ancho chile powder, 2 tbsp.
Crushed red pepper, 2 tsp.
Ground coriander, 2 tsp.
Ground cumin, 1½ tsp.

1 Stir together all ingredients in a small bowl. Place in an airtight container and store at room temperature up to 1 month. About ¼ cup

Note: Ancho chiles are dried poblanos.

Shawarma Spice Blend

"This is my absolute favorite for sandwiches (page 84). You can buy a blend online or make this simple one and keep it around. Aleppo pepper and sumac are sold at Penzey's or Williams-Sonoma."

Ground cardamom, ¼ cup
Ground allspice, 2 Tbsp.
Ground sumac, 2 Tbsp.
Granulated garlic, 1½ Tbsp.
Kosher salt, 1 Tbsp.
Freshly ground black pepper, 1 Tbsp.
Aleppo pepper, 1 tsp.
Sugar, 1 tsp.

1 Stir together all ingredients in a small bowl. Store at room temperature in an airtight container up to 2 months. ½ cup

Za'atar Spice Blend

"This herbaceous Middle Eastern concoction has distinctive notes of sesame and tangy sumac. It is traditionally sprinkled on flat bread or over hummus."

Sesame seeds, ¼ cup lightly toasted
Ground sumac, ½ cup
Dried thyme, 2 Tbsp.
Dried oregano, 2 Tbsp.
Dried marjoram, 2 Tbsp.
Kosher salt, 1 Tbsp.

1 Process sesame seeds in a blender until finely ground.

2 Stir together sesame seeds and remaining ingredients. Store in an airtight container at room temperature up to 1 month. 1¼ cups

Berbere Spice Blend

"Though this has Ethiopian origins, I first tasted this spice combination on a trip to the Atlas Mountains of Morocco. It uses native herbs and chiles not commonly found elsewhere, but this rendition tastes pretty close to the real deal."

Paprika, 3 Tbsp.
Crushed red pepper, 1 Tbsp.
Ground ginger, 1 Tbsp.
Cumin seeds, 2 tsp.
Ground turmeric, 1 tsp.
Kosher salt, 1 tsp.
Fenugreek seeds, 1 tsp.
Coriander seeds, 1 tsp.
Ground cardamom, 1 tsp.
Ground cinnamon, ½ tsp.
Whole allspice, ½ tsp.
Black peppercorns, ½ tsp.
Whole cloves, 8

1 Combine all ingredients in a small skillet. Cook over medium-high heat, stirring constantly, until toasted. Cool completely.

2 Process spice mixture in a blender until finely ground. Store at room temperature in an airtight container up to 3 months. ½ cup

Technique: Toasting spices brings out their flavors. Heat an 8-inch frying pan over medium-high heat. Add the spices and stir until they begin to release their fragrance and are just toasted, about 30 seconds to 1 minute. Transfer to a plate to cool, then grind in a spice grinder. Or do what I do—buy a cheap coffee grinder and dedicate it to grinding spices.

Aioli Series

"The French have Aioli, the Spaniards have Romesco, and we Americans love our mayonnaise. Why so popular? I think it's because aioli accentuates the flavor of any local cuisine. It cuts through sharp flavors, and the creamy texture is irresistible. Emulsifying ingredients by using an egg yolk as the binder is a classic technique I still use, and one for you to learn for sure. A food processor or blender works really well instead of a whisk for this."

Basic Aioli

"Like mayonnaise, aioli is an emulsified sauce, though the kick of minced garlic hints at its Mediterranean roots."

Egg yolk, 1
Fresh lemon juice, 2 tsp.
Kosher salt, ½ tsp.

Freshly ground black pepper, ¼ tsp.
Garlic, 1 clove pressed
Canola oil, 1 cup

1 Whisk together first 5 ingredients in a medium bowl. Whisking rapidly, slowly pour in oil in a thin stream; whisk until thick. 1 cup

Beat egg yolk with lemon juice, seasonings, and garlic, then gradually **add** oil in a steady stream. **Whisk** well until oil is incorporated and mixture is light and creamy.

emulsion (ih-MUHL-shuhn) n. A smooth mixture of two liquids that normally don't mix, such as oil and water. Emulsification is achieved by slowly adding one ingredient into the other while rapidly whisking.

Note: These aioli recipes contain raw eggs. People at risk for foodborne illnesses should avoid eating raw eggs.

Spicy Aioli

"The sriracha sauce found in American supermarkets is like traditional hot sauce on steroids. It has a garlicky flavor and provides sweet heat."

Egg yolks, 2
Garlic, 2 cloves pressed
Rice vinegar, 1 Tbsp.
Sriracha sauce, 1 Tbsp.
Kosher salt, ⅛ tsp.
Freshly ground black pepper, ⅛ tsp.
Canola oil, 1 cup

1 Whisk together first 6 ingredients in a medium bowl. Add oil in a slow, steady stream, whisking until blended and smooth. 1 cup

Curry Aioli

"Curry powder is a Western creation that blends spices commonly used in Indian cooking. It lends an exotic flavor and lovely golden hue to aioli."

Egg yolk, 1
Garlic, 2 cloves pressed
Curry powder, 1 Tbsp.
Mango chutney, 2 Tbsp.
Kosher salt, ½ tsp.
Canola oil, 1 cup

1 Whisk together first 5 ingredients in a medium bowl. Add oil in a slow, steady stream, whisking until blended and smooth. 1 cup

Chipotle Aioli

"Jalapeño peppers that have been smoked are called chipotles. They can be found dried or canned with adobo sauce, a vinegar-based marinade."

Egg yolk, 1
Garlic, 2 cloves pressed
Canned chipotle peppers in adobo sauce, 2 minced
Adobo sauce from can, 2 tsp.
Fresh lemon juice, 2 tsp.
Kosher salt, ½ tsp.
Freshly ground black pepper, ¼ tsp.
Canola oil, 1 cup

1 Whisk together first 7 ingredients in a medium bowl. Add oil in a slow, steady stream, whisking until blended and smooth. 1 cup

Condiments

"I'm a saucy guy. What better way to layer flavor than in slathers, spreads, and drizzles? My versions of these typical condiments are unique and bold. Each one infuses food with an unexpected burst of flavor that wows."

Todd's Spiced Ketchup

"Whip up a batch of this, and you'll never go back to the squirt bottle, my friend."

Unsalted butter, 1 Tbsp.
White onions, 2 diced (about 4 cups)
Diced tomatoes, 1 (14.5-oz.) can

Brown sugar, ½ cup firmly packed
White vinegar, ½ cup
Ground allspice, 1 tsp.

1 Melt butter in a large skillet over medium heat. Add onions; cook, stirring occasionally, 23 minutes or until caramel colored.

2 Stir in tomatoes and remaining ingredients. Reduce heat to medium low, and cook 30 minutes or until reduced by half.

3 Remove mixture from heat, and cool completely. Process in a blender until smooth. Cover and chill thoroughly. 2⅔ cups

Barbecue Sauce

"Zesty and addictive, this classic 'cue sauce gets an Asian flair with sesame, soy sauce, and hoisin."

Vegetable oil, 1 Tbsp.
Onion, 1 cup diced
Garlic, 2 cloves chopped
Ketchup, 1½ cups
Soy sauce, ¼ cup
Dark sesame oil, 1 Tbsp.

Honey, 1 Tbsp.
Cider vinegar, 1 Tbsp.
Hoisin sauce, 1 Tbsp.
Ground ginger, 1½ tsp.
Freshly ground black pepper, ¼ tsp.

1 Heat vegetable oil in a medium saucepan over medium heat. Add onion and garlic; sauté 5 minutes or until tender. Add ¼ cup water, ketchup, and remaining ingredients. Bring to a boil; reduce heat, and simmer, uncovered, 10 minutes. Let cool slightly.

2 Process sauce in a blender until smooth. 2 cups

Mustard Relish

"On a burger or hot dog, this relish reigns supreme."

Dill pickles, ½ cup diced

Dijon mustard, ½ cup

Honey, ½ cup

1 Stir together all ingredients in a medium bowl until blended. 1½ cups

TE Special Sauce

"I put this on everything, but I especially love it on my Game Day Sliders (page 170). Make a batch and keep it in the fridge for a few weeks."

Mayonnaise, 1 cup

Ketchup, 1 cup

Dill pickles, 1 cup finely diced

1 Stir together all ingredients in a bowl until blended. Cover and chill up to 2 weeks. 3 cups

Caper Tartar Sauce

"Easy sauces like this elevate basic dishes in no time. And trust me—everyone you're cooking for will appreciate the special touch. I slather this all over fish in tacos, spread it on sandwiches, and even dip my French fries in it. Yum!"

Mayonnaise, ½ cup

Capers, 4 tsp. drained

Red onion, 2 tsp. minced

Fresh cilantro, 2 tsp. minced

Fresh lemon juice, 2 tsp.

1 Stir together all ingredients in a bowl until blended. Cover and chill. ½ cup

Parmigiano-Reggiano

" Parmigiano-Reggiano is one of my great loves. Growing up with an Italian momma, I experienced the real thing at an early age. There was always a huge wedge in our fridge, but I had no idea what a luxury that was. By the age of 5, I was sneaking chunks, assuming you were only allowed to eat it as a processed powder from a green shaker as I'd seen friends do.

You can imagine what a relief it was when I arrived at culinary school to learn that enjoying it by the chunk was encouraged! As I learned to really cook with it, I realized that Parmigiano-Reggiano transforms in taste and texture depending on how you use it. The meaty chunks I snuck as a kid taste completely different from delicate shavings over risotto or fresh pasta. I loved this. It was moody and delicious in every form.

My love affair with this cheese and its country of origin has continued; so when I had the opportunity to tie Parmigiano-Reggiano into my television show "Food Trip," I leapt at it. We called the episode "Fast Cars and Slow Food," with the premise that I would drive a Ferrari on a mission to learn how to make Parmigiano-Reggiano from one of Parma's most established cheesemakers. Nice job, right? I picked out an ultramodern, 21st-century Ferrari at the factory and drove it to Parma, where it felt like I had stepped back in time three hundred years.

They were milking cows on one side of the road. Then, just like they've been doing for hundreds of years, they transported the milk to the other side of the road to make the cheese. Then they let it sit for 6 to 24 months to age. If they are lucky and the cows produce enough milk, they'll get 24 wheels of Parmigiano a day. It really is slow food! After seeing it made, I appreciate why they call it the noblest of cheeses. And my trip to Parma taught me the most important lesson of all: Respect this ingredient and accept no substitutes when you're cooking. Promise me you'll use the real deal when I call for it in this book."

How To Serve It

Parmigiano-Reggiano really does taste different depending on how you prepare it. Here are my favorite ways:

• Place a big chunk of Parmigiano-Reggiano on a cutting board. Scatter a few slices of grilled bread around it. Put out a bowl of your favorite olive oil for dipping, some artisanal apricot and fig confituras, and maybe a little honey for drizzling. Oh, and don't forget freshly cracked black pepper. Let guests cut off chunks of the cheese themselves and experiment with the combinations.

• Grate it over any of your favorite pasta dishes or risottos. I like using a really fine rasp to create tiny shreds that melt into the warm dish for serving.

• Shave off slices with a vegetable peeler to layer over thinly sliced fennel and citrus, beef carpaccio, or a pizza fresh from the oven.

How To Store

Though more readily available nowadays, Parmigiano-Reggiano is still expensive, so take care of your investment so you don't end up with a piece that's as hard as a rock in a few days. It is also prone to absorb odors from other foods, so I wrap mine very tightly in butcher paper, then wrap it in a really tight layer of plastic wrap. I keep it in my meat and cheese drawer. Every time I use some, I rewrap it so it is fresh to the last chunk, shaving, or crumble.

Global Flavors

"I rely a lot on herbaceous green sauces and creamy vegetable-based ones to add that final flavor burst to a recipe. Here are a few of my favorite combinations."

My Favorite Pesto

"Genovese in origin, pesto lends itself to many interpretations, so feel free to tinker with the ingredients. Walnuts, arugula, and parsley can all stand in with great results. Pesto keeps in the fridge for a week with a thin layer of olive oil poured over the top, or it can be frozen in an airtight container for several months."

Garlic, 3 cloves
Parmigiano-Reggiano cheese, ¾ cup freshly grated
Pine nuts, ½ cup

Fresh basil leaves, 2 cups firmly packed
Kosher salt, 1 tsp.
Freshly ground black pepper, ¼ tsp.
Extra virgin olive oil, ⅔ cup

❶ With processor running, drop garlic through food chute. Process until minced. Add cheese, pine nuts, and 2 Tbsp. water to garlic. Process until a thick paste forms. Add basil, salt, and pepper. With processor running, pour oil through food chute in a slow, steady stream. Process until smooth. 1½ cups

Note: Store leftover pesto in refrigerator, covered with ⅓ cup more olive oil to prevent browning.

Chimichurri

"I've spent enough time in Argentina to see the resurgence of gaucho (Argentinian cowboy) cooking, the tango, and a few other things. They serve their most inexpensive cuts of beef grilled and topped with chimichurri, which is like an explosion of fresh herbs and pungent flavors. Use this sauce on seafood, nachos, and tacos, or as a condiment to drizzle on any sandwich that needs a hit of flavor."

Garlic, 2 cloves
Fresh parsley sprigs, 1 cup firmly packed
Olive oil, ½ cup
Red wine vinegar, ⅓ cup
Fresh cilantro sprigs, ¼ cup firmly packed

Crushed red pepper, ¾ tsp.
Kosher salt, ½ tsp.
Ground cumin, ½ tsp.
Freshly ground black pepper, ¼ tsp.

❶ With processor running, drop garlic through food chute. Process until minced. Add parsley and remaining ingredients; process until smooth. 1 cup

Avocado Crema

"I'm addicted to avocado's creamy texture and versatility. The fruit shines on its own with a little salt and olive oil, and is a wonderful base for Asian, Latin, and European flavor combinations. This crema is the perfect topping for fish tacos (page 188). Just do me a favor—look for ripe avocados that give a little when pressed with a thumb."

Avocados, 4
Sour cream, ¾ cup
Fresh lime juice, 2 Tbsp.
Ground cumin, 1½ tsp.

Ground coriander, 1½ tsp.
Kosher salt, 1 tsp.
Freshly ground black pepper, ½ tsp.

1 Cut avocados in half. Scoop avocado pulp into bowl of a food processor. Add sour cream and remaining ingredients; process until smooth. 2¾ cups

Corn Raita

"The inspiration for this recipe is from the classic Indian condiment, raita. The addition of corn gives it new personality. Toasting the corn draws out its lovely sweetness and lends texture to the spread. Grill the corn whole and then cut the kernels off the cob or as per the instructions below. I keep a batch of this simple recipe on hand in the fridge to add to countless dishes, but I usually end up eating it one spoonful at a time on its own. Try a few spoonfuls on a skirt steak or slathered in a pita sandwich. Nirvana!"

Fresh corn kernels, 2 cups
Plain Greek yogurt, 2 cups
Fresh cilantro leaves, 2 Tbsp. chopped
Ground cumin, 1 tsp.
Kosher salt, ½ tsp

Freshly ground black pepper, ¼ tsp.
Red onion, 2 Tbsp. finely chopped
Jalapeño pepper, 1 seeded and minced
    (optional)

1 Heat a large well-seasoned cast-iron skillet over high heat. Add corn to pan; cook 1 minute without stirring. Stir and cook 2 more minutes or until corn is beginning to brown. Transfer corn to a plate; cool completely.

2 Stir together yogurt and next 4 ingredients in a medium bowl. Fold in corn and onion. Add jalapeño pepper, if desired. 3 cups

Tomatoes

"I am maniacal about fresh tomatoes and enjoy them myriad ways throughout their growing season. I like to showcase them when they are perfectly ripe and juicy in my Brandywine Tomato Stacks (page 76) or give them a smoky char to serve on pizzas and whirl into sauces. When the season ends, I turn to my favorite canned tomatoes from San Marzano, with their perfect balance of flavor and acidity."

Roasted Tomatoes

"Roasting plump Roma tomatoes concentrates their sweet tomato goodness. I use these in my Pan-Seared Tuna with Olive Vinaigrette and Roasted Tomatoes (page 190)."

Extra virgin olive oil, ¼ cup
Garlic, 1 Tbsp. minced
Kosher salt, 1 tsp.
Freshly ground black pepper, ½ tsp.
Plum tomatoes, 12 halved lengthwise
Fresh thyme sprigs, 6
Fresh rosemary sprigs, 2

1 Preheat oven to 425°. Combine all ingredients in a large bowl, tossing to coat with oil. Spread tomato mixture, skin sides up for tomatoes, on a large rimmed baking sheet.

2 Bake at 425° for 30 minutes or until tomato skins begin to brown and tomatoes are soft. 6 servings

Note: Toss into pasta and salads, or place on top of a pizza.

Quick and Luscious Tomato Sauce

"I can't count how many times I have made this sauce or how many times my mom or grandmother made it for me…thousands and thousands, I am sure. It is certain to become part of your repertoire. Fresh ripe tomatoes are beautiful on a skirt steak or slathered in a pita sandwich, provided you remove the skins by quickly blanching, shocking in ice water, and peeling (see below). But, when a stand-in for fresh is required, San Marzanos taste like summertime in a can."

Garlic, 4 cloves very thinly sliced
Extra virgin olive oil, ¾ cup
Whole ripe tomatoes, 3½ lb. peeled and coarsely chopped*
Kosher salt, ½ tsp.
Fresh basil leaves, ¾ cup loosely packed (about 20 leaves) torn

1 Cook garlic in olive oil in a medium skillet over medium-low heat, stirring often, 10 minutes. (Do not brown garlic.) Stir in tomatoes and salt. Bring to a boil; reduce heat, and simmer, uncovered, 15 minutes. Stir in basil. About 2 qt.

*Substitute 2 (28-ounce) cans undrained and chopped San Marzano tomatoes.

Peel tomatoes by cutting a small X at the base of each, then drop them into a pot of boiling water just until the skins begin to loosen, about 10 to 15 seconds. **Remove** the tomatoes with a slotted spoon and transfer to an ice bath. **Peel** by gently slipping off the loose skins.

A.C.G.

"A.C.G. is my code for anchovies, capers, and garlic, a combination of flavors that is the essence of my Italian upbringing. These three staples were always in my great-grandmother Bettina Vergara's pantry. Her daughter (my grandmother, Giulietta) and my mother, Patrizia, carried on the tradition of using these three ingredients as the foundation of their home cooking. In fact, I ate anchovies so often as a child that I can't even remember the first time I tried one!

People seem to have a love-hate relationship with anchovies. In my opinion, they are one of the most delicious and versatile ingredients to work with in Mediterranean cooking. When cooked down and caramelized, anchovies infuse a dish with a distinctive saltiness and an almost indescribable, wildly earthy quality that the Japanese call 'umami.' When cooked with capers and garlic, something otherworldly takes place and the flavor of a dish is elevated. You don't have to overload on these three ingredients to experience their magic. Restraint is the good cook's secret. As you begin to cook with anchovies, you'll realize that the nuance of flavor they lend to a dish is difficult to replicate with any other ingredients.

In addition to my A.C.G. Tomato Sauce on the following page, I love this medley folded into compound butter (page 18). You can also simply cook the anchovies, capers, and garlic in olive oil, then pour the A.C.G.-infused oil over a grilled steak. In case any lingering doubt remains, A.C.G. is one of my favorite combinations on Earth. Once you've experienced it, I think you'll see why I consider it to be the Holy Grail of Mediterranean cooking."

A.C.G. Sauce

"Many cultures have unique *soffritos* that define their type of cooking. Simply put, a soffrito is a combination of finely chopped ingredients that are cooked down and used as a base flavor. Spaniards have their version (tomato, onions, garlic), Italians have theirs (onions, celery, carrots, garlic, parsley), but anchovies, capers, and garlic is all mine! Don't turn your nose up at anchovies. I swear I'll base a show or book on just these three ingredients some day. Stir this medley into hot pasta or vinaigrettes, or toss with roasted potatoes or cooked vegetables. The uses are endless."

Extra virgin olive oil, ⅔ cup
Garlic, 6 cloves very thinly sliced
Anchovy fillets, 6 rinsed and coarsely
  chopped
Capers, 2 Tbsp. rinsed

1 Combine all ingredients in a medium skillet. Cook over medium-low heat 3 minutes, pressing anchovies into pan with back of a wooden spoon until a paste forms. (Do not let garlic brown.) About ¾ cup

Note: To make A.C.G. Tomato Sauce, stir ½ tsp. kosher salt, ¼ tsp. freshly ground black pepper, ⅛ tsp. crushed red pepper, and 3 cups diced tomatoes (about 1½ lbs.) with the A.C.G. Sauce and simmer 20 to 25 minutes until tomatoes are broken down and sauce is smooth. Serve over cooked pasta and garnish with torn fresh basil leaves.

Pizza Dough

"This is the foundation of so many wonderful preparations—pizzas, flatbreads, sandwiches. I prefer a wetter dough than most and like my finished crust to have a bit of chew. Turn to the whole-wheat dough when you want something more dense and flavorful."

Pizza Dough

Active dry yeast, 1 (¼-oz.) envelope
Sugar, ¼ cup
Warm water (100° to 110°), 1⅔ cups, divided

Olive oil, ¾ cup
Kosher salt, 1 Tbsp.
All-purpose flour, 5 cups

1 Combine yeast, sugar, and 1 cup warm water in a 2-cup glass measuring cup; stir until sugar dissolves. Let stand 5 minutes.

2 Combine yeast mixture, remaining ⅔ cup warm water, oil, and salt in bowl of a heavy-duty electric stand mixer. Add flour; beat at low speed, using dough hook attachment, 10 minutes, until dough pulls together and becomes soft and smooth.

3 Cover bowl of dough with lightly greased plastic wrap, and let rise in a warm place (85°), free from drafts, 1 hour and 30 minutes or until doubled in bulk.

4 Punch dough down. Turn dough out onto a lightly floured surface; divide into 4 portions. Proceed as directed in recipe. 4 (12- x 10-inch) oblong pizza crusts

Whole-Wheat Pizza Dough

Active dry yeast, 1 (¼-oz.) envelope
Molasses, 1 Tbsp.
Warm water (100° to 110°), 1⅔ cups, divided
Honey, 2 Tbsp.

Olive oil, ¼ cup
Kosher salt, 1 Tbsp. plus 2 tsp.
Whole-wheat flour, 2 cups
Wheat germ, ½ cup
All-purpose flour, 2 cups

1 Combine yeast, molasses, and 1 cup warm water in a 2-cup glass measuring cup; stir until molasses dissolves. Let stand 5 minutes.

2 Combine yeast mixture, remaining ⅔ cup warm water, honey, oil, and salt in bowl of a heavy-duty electric stand mixer. Add whole-wheat flour and wheat germ, and beat at low speed, using dough hook attachment, 2 minutes. Add 1½ cups all-purpose flour; beat 8 minutes. Gradually add remaining flour, if needed, until dough pulls together and becomes soft and smooth.

3 Cover bowl of dough with lightly greased plastic wrap, and let rise in a warm place (85°), free from drafts, 1 hour and 30 minutes or until doubled in bulk.

4 Punch dough down. Turn dough out onto a lightly floured surface; divide into 4 portions. Proceed as directed in recipe. 4 (12- x 10-inch) oblong pizza crusts

Homemade Pasta

Fresh Semolina Pasta

Unbleached all-purpose flour, 2 cups
Semolina flour, ½ cup
Kosher salt, 1 tsp.

Large eggs, 3
Egg yolks, 2

1 Combine flours and salt on a work surface; make a well in center. Place eggs and egg yolks in center of flour well. Whisk eggs with a fork, gradually stirring in flour from bottom of well. Push some flour from sides of well into the center as mixture thickens. Continue whisking with fork until mixture becomes very stiff.

2 Knead dough on a lightly floured surface 10 minutes or until smooth. Cover ball of dough with plastic wrap; chill 30 minutes before use. Roll out as required in your recipe. 1-lb. dough

"I'm a fresh pasta fanatic and am on a mission to preserve the pasta-making art. This recipe uses semolina, which adds some tooth to the silky texture of the noodles. Once you master pasta making, you can cut fettuccine to serve with my Bolognese (page 209) or pappardelle to top with my Dreamy Mushroom Sauce (page 130). Or, simply cut spaghetti to pair with my basic Quick and Luscious Tomato Sauce (page 31). The key to matching pasta with sauces is to remember: The thicker the cut of pasta, the thicker the sauce."

Cocktails and Appetizers

Aren't cocktails a great way to build up to a meal? They are meant to prime your palate for the experience ahead. They should be light, crisp, and cold to enhance your appetite. I try to serve a cocktail that hints at what's to come—my Watermelon Cooler sets the tone for a night of casual, grilled food. Pear Cider warms people to the idea of my Prime Rib Chili and an easy day of football watching.

As far as appetizers go, I put few rules around this course. Appetizers can either be an introduction to the theme of the food that will be served for dinner or highlight an ingredient or two that is in season. And if you're really excited about creating a special appetizer for friends, you can certainly scale down the entrée so it's not much bigger than the appetizer; then guests aren't stuffed, just satisfied. Cocktails and appetizers should be inviting—like tantalizing little offerings that celebrate coming together—and whet the appetite for the main attraction.

Granulated sugar, ½ cup

Simple Syrup

1 Combine ½ cup water and sugar in a small saucepan; bring to a boil, reduce heat, and simmer 2 minutes. Remove from heat. Pour syrup into a small jar. Cover and store in refrigerator. ¾ cup

Microwave Simple Syrup: To make a quick simple syrup, stir together 2 Tbsp. each water and sugar in a small bowl. Microwave at HIGH 30 seconds; stir until sugar dissolves. Cool.

Sage Simple Syrup: Add 4 large fresh sage leaves to sugar mixture before bringing to a boil.

Rosemary Simple Syrup: Substitute turbinado sugar for granulated sugar. Add 3 (5- to 6-inch) fresh rosemary sprigs to sugar mixture before bringing to a boil.

Watermelon, 5 cups seeded cubes
Light rum, 1 cup
Club soda, 3 Tbsp. chilled
Simple Syrup (above), 2 Tbsp.
Garnish: melon balls

Watermelon Cooler

1 Process watermelon cubes in a blender until liquefied; strain and measure 1½ cups liquid into a small pitcher. Stir in rum, club soda, and Simple Syrup. Serve over ice. Garnish, if desired. 4 servings

"This guava margarita is a delicious cocktail tailor-made for sipping with highly seasoned foods. For the tastiest margaritas, splurge on top-quality tequila. I promise you'll taste the difference—and feel better the next day!"

Guava Margarita

1 Combine first 5 ingredients in a large pitcher; cover and chill. Serve over ice. Garnish, if desired. 4 servings

Note: To serve with citrus salt, rub the rim of the glass with the cut side of a lime, invert the glass in a container of margarita salt mixed with finely grated lime zest, and give a twist to coat.

Guava nectar, 2 cups
Silver tequila, 1½ cups
Fresh orange juice, 1 cup
Cointreau, ¼ cup
Simple Syrup (page 40), ¼ cup
Garnish: lime slices

"This is a fun, festive drink for a casual summer party. I love to serve this along with some of my casual appetizers, such as Fire-Roasted Eggplant (page 48) and Corn Raita (page 29). Be sure to put a few pieces of fruit in each glass. After a long soak in the wine, the flavor of the fruit is amazing!"

Fresh strawberries, 20 halved
Oranges, 2 cut into ¼-inch-thick slices
Rosé wine, 1 (750-milliliter) bottle
Brandy, ½ cup
Orange liqueur, ½ cup
Simple Syrup (page 40), ¼ cup
Ginger ale, ½ cup

Olives' Rosé Sangria

1 Place strawberry halves and orange slices in a large pitcher. Add Rosé wine and next 4 ingredients; stir gently, and chill 24 hours.

2 Serve over ice. 6 servings

Note: We tested with Grand Marnier orange liqueur and Spanish rosado wine.

Mango chunks, ¾ cup fresh or frozen
  thawed
Fresh mint leaves, 1 cup packed
Simple Syrup (page 40), ½ cup
Light rum, 1½ cups
Club soda, 1 cup
Fresh lime juice, ½ cup
Garnishes: fresh mint sprigs and mango slices

"Mojitos! It's difficult to imagine a more lively or refreshing drink. My addition of mango boosts the island vibe. To make mango puree, simply throw some fresh or frozen (but thawed) mango in a blender until it's smooth."

Mango Mojito

1 Process mango in a blender until pureed to measure ½ cup.

2 Place mint and Simple Syrup in a pitcher. Gently press leaves against sides of pitcher with back of a spoon to release flavor. Remove mint, using a slotted spoon. Add mango puree, rum, club soda, and lime juice; stir. Serve over ice. Garnish, if desired. 4 to 6 servings

Variation: Substitute strawberries for the mango chunks, or omit the puree and add a splash more lime juice and club soda for a classic mojito.

Slice: With a sharp knife, make a lengthwise cut about an inch off center, just grazing the side of the pit. Repeat on other side of the fruit, and trim off the flesh left around the pit. **Score:** Carefully score the cut sides of the mango halves in a crisscross pattern through the flesh. **Remove:** Bend the peel back so the cubes of fruit pop out; cut across, next to the peel, to remove the cubes.

"Amanda Haas, my sidekick on this book, has many talents. Among them is that she is a gifted mixologist. She won me over with her signature shaken-not-stirred cocktail. Pomegranates are all the rage now because they are loaded with antioxidants, but the juice can taste medicinal on its own. Combined with cranberry juice, vodka, and orange liqueur, it shines in this (dare-I-say 'healthy?') cocktail."

Amanda's Pomegranate Martini

1 Fill a martini shaker half full of ice. Add first 4 ingredients in the order given. Cover with lid; shake vigorously until thoroughly chilled. Remove lid; strain into 2 martini glasses. Garnish, if desired. Serve immediately. 2 servings

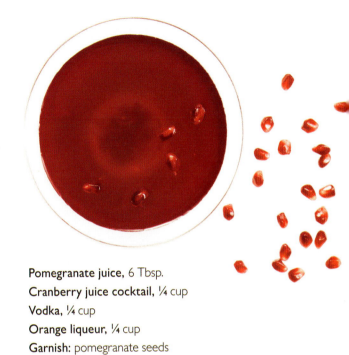

Pomegranate juice, 6 Tbsp.
Cranberry juice cocktail, ¼ cup
Vodka, ¼ cup
Orange liqueur, ¼ cup
Garnish: pomegranate seeds

"This comforting cocktail is pure autumn in a glass. I like to pair it with my Prime Rib Chili (page 174). Look for high-quality pear nectar alongside other jarred juices or in a carton in the juice aisle. Ginger beer is available at most grocery and package stores."

Pear Cider

1 Fill 2 highball glasses with ice. Pour 3 Tbsp. bourbon, 3 Tbsp. nectar, and ¼ cup ginger beer over ice in each glass. Garnish, if desired. Serve immediately. 2 servings

Bourbon, 6 Tbsp.
Pear nectar, 6 Tbsp.
Ginger beer, ½ cup
Garnish: pear slices

43

"Who mixes gin with Champagne, you ask? I do! Because it's served in a Champagne glass, it's an unexpected surprise to taste the gin and lemon. This is an ideal start to an elegant dinner party. Or maybe a raucous one…"

Imperial Gin Fizz

Gin, ¾ cup

Fresh lemon juice, ¼ cup

Simple Syrup (page 40), 2 Tbsp.

Ice cubes, 2 cups

Champagne, 1 cup

❶ Place gin, lemon juice, Simple Syrup, and ice in a martini shaker. Cover with lid, and shake vigorously until thoroughly chilled. Remove lid, and strain, pouring ¼ cup into each of 4 Champagne flutes. Top each with ¼ cup Champagne. Serve immediately. 4 servings

"I'm not typically a brown liquor kind of guy, but I could drink these until the cows come home! It's something about the combination of the bourbon spiked with orange, apple, and ginger sweetened with maple syrup. It is scarily sippable."

Kentucky Maple

1 Combine first 4 ingredients in a martini shaker filled with ice. Squeeze juice from orange slice over mixture, and discard. Cover with lid; shake vigorously until thoroughly chilled. Remove lid; strain into a martini glass. Garnish, if desired. Serve immediately. 1 serving

Bourbon, ¼ cup
Apple cider, ¼ cup
Ginger beer, 3 Tbsp.
Maple syrup, 2¼ tsp.
Orange, 1 (¼-inch-thick) slice
Garnish: lady apple,
   1 (¼-inch-thick) slice

"Another cool twist on a classic. This one is a surprise on the palate, with earthy sage and the brightness of lime. If you decide to garnish, clap the sage leaves between your palms before adding them to the cocktail. This bruises the leaves, releasing the natural oils, aroma, and flavor."

Old Sage Martini

1 Combine gin, lime juice, and Sage Simple Syrup in a martini shaker filled with ice. Cover with lid; shake vigorously until thoroughly chilled. Remove lid; strain into martini glasses. Garnish, if desired. Serve immediately. 2 servings

Gin, ⅔ cup
Fresh lime juice, ¼ cup
Sage Simple Syrup (page 40), 2 Tbsp.
Garnish: fresh sage leaves

Dried Turkish figs, 6
Lillet, 7 Tbsp., divided
Light rum, 3 Tbsp.
Rosemary Simple Syrup (page 40), 1 Tbsp.
Ice cubes, 1 cup
Garnish: dried fig, fresh rosemary sprig

"Figs and rosemary lend an autumnal flavor to this feisty little libation. Lillet is a citrusy spirit that adds even more character to the pronounced flavor medley. Sip on this awhile, and you may break into a rap as the name suggests."

Notorious F.I.G.

1 Process figs and 1 Tbsp. Lillet in a food processor 30 seconds or until figs are pureed.

2 Combine 1 Tbsp. fig puree (reserve remaining puree for another use), remaining 6 Tbsp. Lillet, rum, Rosemary Simple Syrup, and ice in a martini shaker. Cover with lid, and shake vigorously until thoroughly chilled. Pour into an old-fashioned glass. Garnish, if desired. 1 serving

"No need to wait for a horse race to enjoy a julep. This cousin of the classic mint julep muddles juicy, aromatic peaches with the mint. Look for sweet-smelling, just-picked peaches. When peach season has passed, mix up a classic julep instead. Or turn to frozen peaches. Frozen peaches that have been thawed are better than lackluster, mealy ones sold as 'fresh' in the market."

Savannah Julep

1 Place mint leaves and peach quarter in a highball glass. Press leaves and peach against sides of glass. Add bourbon, Simple Syrup, and lime juice to glass; fill with ice. Pour mixture into a martini shaker. Cover with lid; shake vigorously until thoroughly chilled. Remove lid; return mixture to highball glass. Garnish, if desired. 1 serving

Fresh mint leaves, 6
Fresh peach, 1 quarter peeled
Bourbon, 6 Tbsp.
Simple Syrup (page 40), 2 Tbsp.
Lime, ½ medium juiced
Garnish: fresh mint sprig

"Dark and Stormy cocktails are good, but Dark and Stormiers are even better! Pineapple juice is the secret to this drink, and it's a great complement to the ginger beer and rums. Ginger beer, a close cousin to ginger ale, is also nonalcoholic, yet has a stronger bite and is great as a mixer in cocktails. I dare you to drink just one of these!"

Dark and Stormier

1 Fill a highball glass with ice. Pour light rum and next 3 ingredients over ice in the order given. Squeeze orange slice over mixture; drop it in for garnish. 1 serving

Light rum, ¼ cup
Dark rum, ¼ cup
Pineapple juice, 3 Tbsp.
Ginger beer, 6 Tbsp.
Orange, 1 (¼-inch-thick) slice

olive oil + onion + garlic

Lentil and Berbere Dip

Dried red or yellow lentils, ½ cup
Olive oil, 2 tsp.
Onion, ¼ cup diced
Garlic, 4 cloves minced

Berbere Spice Blend (page 21), 1 tsp.
Chicken broth, 1 cup
Pita squares or naan

1 Sort then rinse lentils; drain.

2 Heat oil in a medium saucepan over medium-high heat. Add onion and garlic; sauté 3 minutes. Add Berbere Spice Blend; sauté 1 minute. Reduce heat to medium. Add chicken broth. Stir in lentils; cook 15 minutes or until lentils are tender. Remove from heat, and let cool 30 minutes.

3 Process lentil mixture in a blender 10 seconds or until smooth. Serve with pita squares or naan. 2 cups

Casual Mezze

"In Turkey, North Africa, and Greece, they have it right. Meals are often made from sharing small plates of various dishes. I might serve a trio of dishes with my Olives' Rosé Sangria (page 41) for a communal lunch or a few with before-dinner cocktails to prime the appetite for the meal ahead."

Drink: American Blonde Ale

olive oil + garlic + lemon juice

Fire-Roasted Eggplant

Eggplant, 2 medium halved lengthwise
Olive oil, ¼ cup, divided
Garlic, 3 large cloves halved
Fresh lemon juice, 2 Tbsp.
Tahini, 2 Tbsp.

Kosher salt, ¾ tsp.
Freshly ground black pepper, ⅛ tsp.
Pita chips
Garnish: chopped parsley

1 Preheat grill to 350° to 400° (medium-high) heat. Brush eggplant halves on all sides with 1 Tbsp. oil. Grill, covered with grill lid, 17 minutes or until tender, turning after 10 minutes. Let stand until cool enough to handle.

2 With food processor running, drop garlic through food chute; process until minced. Scoop pulp from eggplant halves, discarding skins; add to garlic. Add lemon juice and next 3 ingredients; process until smooth. With processor running, pour remaining oil in a thin stream through food chute. Process until combined. Serve with pita chips. Garnish, if desired. 2 cups

Dried oregano   +   *ground cinnamon*   +   *olive oil*

Fried Halloumi

All-purpose flour, ¼ cup
Dried oregano, 2 tsp.
Ground cinnamon, ¼ tsp.
Freshly ground black pepper, ¼ tsp.
Halloumi cheese, 8 oz. cut into
   1-inch cubes

Olive oil, ¼ cup
Quick and Luscious Tomato Sauce
  (page 31), ½ cup

1 Place flour in a shallow dish. Stir together oregano, cinnamon, and pepper in a medium bowl. Dredge cheese cubes in flour, shaking off excess.

2 Heat olive oil over medium-high heat in a 10-inch skillet. Fry cheese cubes in hot oil 2 minutes on each side or until browned. Drain on paper towels.

3 Add fried cheese cubes to spice mixture, tossing to coat. Serve with Quick and Luscious Tomato Sauce. 4 servings

goat cheese + garlic + shallots + white wine

"Fondue is back big time. It's naturally easy to socialize around fondue because it's self-service and the ingredients used for dipping suit many tastes. Making a roux is the key to preventing cheesy sauces like this from breaking or looking curdled. Learn the technique now and use it forever."

Unsalted butter, 6 Tbsp.
All-purpose flour, 6 Tbsp.
Shallots, 2 Tbsp. chopped
Garlic, 2 tsp. minced
Olive oil, 2 tsp.
Dry white wine, ¼ cup
Heavy cream, 3 cups
Goat cheese, 20 oz. crumbled
Kosher salt, ⅜ tsp.
Freshly ground black pepper, ⅛ tsp.
Fresh chives, ¼ cup thin diagonal slices
Dippers: toasted bread cubes, dried fig slices, dried date slices, Fuji apple slices

Drink: California Gewürztraminer

Goat Cheese Fondue

❶ Melt butter in a small heavy skillet over low heat; whisk in flour until smooth. Cook, whisking constantly, 2 minutes or until mixture is light brown and has a nutty fragrance. Remove from heat.

❷ Sauté shallots and garlic in olive oil in a medium saucepan over medium heat 3 minutes or until tender. (Do not brown.) Gradually add wine, stirring to loosen particles from bottom of pan. Gradually stir in cream and cheese. Bring to a boil; reduce heat, and simmer 1 minute or until cheese melts. Stir in flour mixture. Cook, stirring constantly, 3 minutes or until smooth and thick. Remove from heat. Stir in salt and pepper.

❸ Transfer fondue to a fondue pot. Sprinkle with chives. Serve with bread cubes, figs, dates, and apple slices. 6 cups (about 12 servings)

Note: A creamy Gorgonzola or Cambozola makes a great alternative to goat cheese.

roux (ROO) n. A cooked mixture of flour and fat that thickens and adds distinctive taste to many dishes. The color and flavor of the roux are determined by how long it cooks. In general, a blond or medium-brown roux is used in sauces or gravies for dark, heavy beef or wild game dishes; it adds a toasted nutty flavor. A dark brown or black roux is used in sauces and gravies for sweet, light meats, such as pork, veal, fish, shellfish, and gumbo.

"This is fiesta food for sure. This zesty queso can be served with tortilla chips, pita, crostini, or a bunch of assorted veggies. It's also a great sauce for enchiladas hot from the oven."

poblano peppers + onion + jalapeño pepper + Oaxaca

Green Chile con Queso

1 Preheat broiler with oven rack 5 inches from heat. Place poblano peppers, skin sides up, on an aluminum foil-lined baking sheet. Broil 10 minutes or until peppers look blistered. Place peppers in a large zip-top plastic freezer bag; seal and let stand 10 minutes to loosen skins. Peel and chop peppers.

2 Heat oil in a medium saucepan over medium heat. Add onion and jalapeño pepper; sauté 3 minutes. Add tomato; sauté 1 minute. Reduce heat to medium; stir in flour. Cook, stirring constantly, 1 minute. Gradually stir in milk. Increase heat to medium-high; cook, stirring constantly, 2 minutes. Remove from heat; add cheeses, roasted peppers, green onions, and salt, stirring until cheeses melt. Serve with tortilla chips. 9 servings

Note: Monterey Jack cheese can be substituted for Oaxaca cheese.

drink: Guava Margarita (page 41)

Poblano peppers, 3 large halved and seeded
Olive oil, 2 Tbsp.
Onion, ½ medium diced (about ¾ cup)
Jalapeño peppers, 2 large seeded and
   minced (about ⅓ cup)
Tomato, 1 medium diced (about 1 cup)
All-purpose flour, 2 Tbsp.
Milk, 1½ cups
Oaxaca (white Mexican cheese),
   ¾ cup (3 oz.) shredded
Monterey Jack cheese, ½ cup (2 oz.)
   shredded
White Cheddar cheese, ½ cup (2 oz.)
   shredded
Green onions, ½ cup sliced
Kosher salt, ½ tsp.
Tortilla chips

"Ceviche is such a simple and delicious way to prepare really fresh fish. The acid in the citrus gives the fish incredible texture and flavor. As you begin to understand how different flavors work in harmony, you will be able to improvise with other herbs and spices to create new spins. Any type of melon that's in season works beautifully here. Tuna and scallops are great stand-ins for the snapper."

citrus juice + red onion + cilantro + jalapeño pepper

Fresh lemon juice, ⅓ cup
Fresh orange juice, ⅓ cup
Fresh lime juice, ⅓ cup
Red onion, 2 Tbsp. finely diced
Fresh cilantro, 1 Tbsp. chopped
Green onions, 1 Tbsp. chopped
Extra virgin olive oil, 1 Tbsp.
Jalapeño pepper, 1 small seeded and finely diced
American red snapper, 1 lb. cut into ¼-inch cubes
Kosher salt, ½ tsp.
Freshly ground black pepper, ¼ tsp.
Cantaloupe, 1 cup finely diced chilled
Avocado Crema (page 29), 2 cups
Garnish: lime wedges

drink: Brut Champagne

Red Snapper and Melon Ceviche

1 Combine first 8 ingredients in a medium bowl. Add snapper, and toss gently. Cover and chill 30 minutes or until fish appears thoroughly cooked. Stir in salt and pepper; add cantaloupe, and toss gently.

2 Spoon about ½ cup ceviche into each of 6 martini glasses. Top each with ⅓ cup Avocado Crema. Garnish, if desired. Serve immediately. 6 servings

ceviche (seh-VEE-chee) n. a Latin American appetizer of very fresh, raw saltwater fish marinated in citrus juice. The acid in the lemon juice firms up the fish texture similar to cooking. (People at risk for foodborne illness should avoid eating raw fish.)

"I've been making tuna crudo for years, and it continues to be a signature item on my menu at Olives. But I love inventing new versions of things, and this one is perfect to make at home. Sesame seeds add texture to the silky tuna, and spicy sriracha lends a little heat. Ask your fishmonger for sushi-grade tuna. Don't be afraid to specify that the piece come from the back of the store instead of the fish case. You'll get the freshest piece, plus you'll get brownie points for knowing your stuff."

Soy sauce or tamari, 2 tsp.
Sesame seeds, 2 tsp., divided
Sriracha sauce, 1½ tsp.
Dark sesame oil, ½ tsp.
Mayonnaise, 2 Tbsp. (optional)
Yellow fin tuna, 1 (4-oz.) fillet cut into
    ½-inch cubes
Cucumber, 4 thin slices

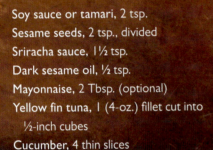

sriracha sauce + *sesame seed* + *dark sesame oil*

Tuna Crudo

1 Stir together soy sauce, 1 tsp. sesame seeds, sriracha sauce, sesame oil, and, if desired, mayonnaise. Add tuna, tossing to coat.

2 Spoon about 2 Tbsp. tuna mixture into each of 4 tiny cups or shot glasses. Top each serving with ¼ tsp. sesame seeds and a cucumber slice. 4 servings

Drink: Oregon Pinot Noir

crudo (KROO-do) n. In Italy, raw fish dressed with olive oil, citrus juice, and/or vinegar. (People at risk for foodborne illness should avoid eating raw fish.)

"Often considered a Sunday morning treat or a bagel's best friend, smoked salmon is a go-to for use in appetizers, too. Serve these sliders at a cocktail party, or enjoy them as a better-than-a-sausage-biscuit morning meal. Find a brand of smoked salmon that you really like and stick with it, as many can be overpoweringly smoky or fishy. Ask your fishmonger for his favorite brands, and see if you can sample a few before purchasing."

lemon + capers + red onion + crème fraîche

Smoked Salmon Sliders

1 Stir together 1 Tbsp. olive oil and next 6 ingredients in a medium bowl. Add salmon and onion, tossing to coat.

2 Heat remaining 2 Tbsp. olive oil in a large nonstick skillet over medium heat. Toast roll halves, cut sides down, in batches in hot olive oil 2 minutes or until golden.

3 Spread cut sides of each roll half with 1 tsp. crème fraîche. Divide salmon mixture evenly among rolls. Top each with 1 piece of lettuce, 1 tomato slice, and a roll top. Place sandwiches on a serving platter. 12 servings

Drink: **Brut Champagne**

Extra virgin olive oil, 3 Tbsp., divided
Chives, ¼ cup finely minced
Lemon zest, 1 tsp.
Capers, 1 Tbsp. rinsed
Kosher salt, ¼ tsp.
Freshly ground black pepper, ¼ tsp.
Fresh lemon juice, ¼ cup
Smoked salmon slices, 12 oz.
Red onion, ½ small thinly sliced
Slider rolls, 12 halved horizontally
Crème fraîche (or sour cream), ½ cup
Butter lettuce, 3 leaves torn into
  4 pieces each
Plum tomatoes, 2 each cut into 6 slices

"Oh boy, do I have opinions on crab cakes! I think a good crab cake is loaded with crabmeat and just barely bound together by other ingredients like mustard, herbs, and crumbs. Whether it's Stone Crab Claws at Joe's in South Beach, whacking Mary-lands along the Chesapeake, Dungeness from the West Coast, or the most amazing King Crab fresh from Alaska, I cannot get enough. Purchase it freshly picked from the shell by the pound from the seafood shop. Steer clear of pasteurized crabmeat, which can have 'off' flavors."

Dijon mustard   +   lemon zest   +   parsley   +   green onion

Crab Cakes

Jumbo lump crabmeat, 1 lb. drained
Large eggs, 2
Panko breadcrumbs, 1 cup
Sour cream, ½ cup
Fresh parsley, 1 Tbsp. finely chopped
Green onions, 1 Tbsp. finely chopped
Dijon mustard, 1 tsp.
Lemon zest, 1 tsp.
Kosher salt, ½ tsp.
Freshly ground black pepper, ¼ tsp.
Vegetable oil
Basic Aioli (page 22)
Garnish: lemon wedges

❶ Pick crabmeat, removing any bits of shell. Whisk eggs in a medium bowl. Stir in panko and next 7 ingredients. Gently stir in crabmeat. Shape crab mixture into 24 (1-inch-thick) small patties. Place on a baking sheet; cover and chill 30 minutes.

❷ Preheat oven to 350°. Line a baking sheet with aluminum foil, and lightly grease foil. Pour oil to depth of ¼ inch into a large skillet. Fry crab cakes in hot oil, in 2 batches, 3 minutes on each side or until dark brown and crisp. Transfer to prepared baking sheet. Bake at 350° for 5 to 7 minutes or until thoroughly heated. Serve with a dollop of Basic Aioli. Garnish, if desired. 6 servings

"Let's face it—food on a stick is fun, and this recipe is undeniably simple and delicious. New England has an enormous Portuguese influence, and years ago, a guy would sell me his family's homemade chorizo, and that's how this simple recipe came about. Try it with more readily available andouille or kielbasa."

Andouille and Cippolini Skewers

1 Soak wooden skewers in water to cover 30 minutes.

2 Preheat oven to 350°. Place onions on a jelly-roll pan. Drizzle with 2 Tbsp. olive oil and balsamic vinegar; sprinkle with salt and pepper, and toss to coat. Bake at 350° for 45 minutes or until tender. Cool 10 minutes. Snip off root ends of onions with kitchen shears.

3 Preheat grill to 350° to 400° (medium-high) heat. Cut sausage diagonally into 24 pieces. Alternately thread 2 pieces sausage and 2 onions on each skewer. Brush skewers with 1 Tbsp. olive oil. Cut bread pieces in half horizontally. Brush remaining 3 Tbsp. olive oil on cut sides of bread.

4 Grill skewers, covered with grill lid, 2 to 3 minutes on each side or until done. Place bread slices, cut sides down, on grill rack; grill 2 minutes or until toasted. Serve skewers with bread and Chimichurri. 6 servings

Drink: Mango Mojito or classic mojito variation (page 42)

Wooden or metal
  skewers, 12 (6-inch)
Cippolini onions,
  24 peeled
Olive oil, 6 Tbsp., divided
Balsamic vinegar, 1 Tbsp.
Kosher salt, 1 tsp.
Freshly ground black pepper, ½ tsp.
Andouille sausage, 1 lb.
French bread baguette, 1 (16-oz.)
  cut diagonally into 6 pieces
Chimichurri (page 28), ½ cup

Bruschetta

"Pronounced 'broo-SKEH-tah,' this is another crowd-pleasing recipe that has infinite variations. The basic idea is to rub a cut tomato onto grilled or toasted bread. The rough and uneven sliced bread 'grates' the tomato while simultaneously absorbing the juices.

The ripeness and flavor of the tomatoes are of course important to the success of this recipe; however, the quality of the bread is key, too. Use a hearty country loaf that you slice yourself—machine-cut will be too thin and too smooth; you need a rougher edge to grate the tomatoes and garlic.

If you use a grill to toast the bread, it will be all the more flavorful; with or without, this simple recipe rocks."

Drink: Italian Pinot Grigio

Catalan-Style Bruschetta
(Pan con Tomate)

Country bread, 6 (¾-inch) slices
Olive oil, ¼ cup
Garlic, 2 cloves halved

Tomato, 1 medium halved
Kosher salt and freshly ground
   black pepper to taste

1 Preheat grill to 350° to 400° (medium-high) heat. Brush both sides of bread with oil. Grill, covered with grill lid, 2 to 3 minutes on each side or until toasted. Rub toast slices on 1 side with cut sides of garlic halves. Rub tomato halves over garlic on bread. Sprinkle with salt and pepper to taste. Serve immediately. 6 servings

Tuscan Style: Rub toast slices with fresh mint sprigs after rubbing with garlic. (You'll need about 10 fresh mint sprigs.) Proceed as directed in recipe.

Gorgonzola: Top each toast slice with about 1 Tbsp. Gorgonzola cheese after sprinkling with salt and pepper.

Tuna and Green Olive: Gently stir together 1 (5-oz.) can chunk light tuna packed in oil, drained and flaked; 1 cup coarsely chopped pitted Spanish olives; ⅓ cup mayonnaise; and 1 tsp. fresh lemon juice in a medium bowl. Rub tomato halves over garlic on bread. Sprinkle with salt and pepper to taste. Spoon 2 Tbsp. tuna mixture onto each toast. Sprinkle tuna mixture with chopped fresh parsley.

grate (GREYT) v. To scrape a piece of food against a coarse, serrated surface until it's reduced to small particles or thin shreds. Grating is similar to shredding; however, grating produces smaller pieces.

Soups, Salads, Sandwiches

A warm bowl of soup, a crunchy salad, and a hearty sandwich are all wonderful by themselves. But serve them together, and I'm in heaven. A cup of soup is such a great primer to dinner, and a bigger bowl is easy sustenance for a hectic weeknight.

Without a doubt, salads are my favorite way to highlight fresh, seasonal produce. I take them beyond the typical tangle of dressed greens by coming up with unique combinations of ingredients that are unexpected, yet work well together. Salads can be meals in their own right, and it's the only time most of us tend to eat raw ingredients. When you don't feel like cooking, what could be better?

I love that you can take garden vegetables, a layer of protein, and pretty much anything else you like and put it between two slices of bread for an entire meal on the go. Forget one-pot meals; sandwiches are no-pot meals that can be suited to every taste. The beauty of this chapter is that you can mix and match the recipes to create easy meals.

"Recently, I spent a day on an avocado farm in California. The farmer picked a sun-ripened avocado for me, cut it in half, and topped it with a sprinkle of salt and a drizzle of extra virgin olive oil. It was the best avocado I've ever tasted in my life. It reminded me that avocados should be eaten only when perfectly ripe and in season, and that the simplest preparation allows them to shine. This soup enhances the natural flavor and creamy texture of the fruit, and can be made a few hours before you'd like to serve it."

Red onion, 1 small chopped

Extra virgin olive oil, 1 Tbsp.

Fresh ginger, 2 tsp. coarsely chopped

Garlic, 1 clove minced

Avocado, 1 large

Cucumber, 1 cup peeled, seeded, and chopped

Fresh lemon juice, 1 Tbsp.

Fresh chives, 2 Tbsp. chopped

Chicken broth, 1½ cups chilled

Crème fraîche, ⅓ cup

Kosher salt, ½ tsp.

Garnish: diced seeded plum tomato

red onion + *ginger* + *cucumber* + *avocado*

Avocado Soup

1 Sauté onion in hot oil in a large nonstick skillet over medium heat 3 minutes. Add ginger and garlic; sauté 1 minute. Remove from heat.

2 Cut avocado in half. Scoop avocado pulp into processor bowl. Add cucumber and lemon juice; process until smooth. Add onion mixture and chives; process until smooth.

3 Pour avocado mixture into a large bowl. Whisk in chicken broth, crème fraîche, and salt. Cover and chill thoroughly.

4 Ladle soup into bowls. Garnish, if desired. 2 servings

Drink: Guava Margarita (page 41) or classic margarita variation

Pit an avocado by slicing all the way around the pit and through both ends of the fruit with a chef's knife. Twist the halves in opposite directions, and pull them apart. Tap the pit with the knife blade, and twist the knife to lift the pit and discard.

"Ripe tomatoes are one of life's great pleasures! (Is it obvious I'm Italian?) When they're ripe, don't over-think the preparation. Grill them before you combine them with a few simple ingredients to create one of the best soups you'll ever taste. Leave a few slices of sourdough bread on your counter overnight to get just the right amount of crust to give this soup some texture."

Plum tomatoes, 12 halved vertically
Red onion, ½ cut into ⅓-inch slices
Extra virgin olive oil, 6 Tbsp., divided
Garlic, 4 large cloves halved
Day-old sourdough bread cubes, 2 cups
Fresh basil leaves, ¾ cup loosely packed
Vegetable broth, 1½ cups
Freshly ground black pepper, ⅛ tsp.
Garnish: small fresh basil leaves

Drink: Czech-Style Pilsner

Grilled Tomato Soup

❶ Heat a grill pan over medium heat. Preheat oven to 400°. Place tomatoes and onion in a large bowl. Drizzle vegetables with 2 Tbsp. oil; toss gently. Place tomato and onion on grill pan; char in batches, 3 minutes on each side or until beginning to blacken. Remove vegetables from grill pan and place on a large rimmed baking sheet. Add garlic cloves to tomato mixture. Bake at 400° for 20 minutes or until garlic is soft and golden. Cool slightly.

❷ Process tomato mixture, bread cubes, and basil leaves in a blender until smooth, stopping to scrape sides as needed. With blender running and center cap removed from lid, pour remaining ¼ cup olive oil through lid. Process until blended. Pour mixture into a large saucepan.

❸ Stir vegetable broth and pepper into tomato mixture. Cook over medium-low heat, stirring occasionally, 5 minutes or until thoroughly heated. Ladle soup into bowls. Garnish, if desired. 4 servings

"So simple, yet so delicious. The combination of alliums—leeks, onions, and garlic—slowly cooked to concentrate their sweetness creates layers of robust flavor not found in a traditional onion soup. Master this technique for making croutons. It's the perfect way to use up stale bread."

leeks + *red onion* + *garlic* + *smoked bacon*

Roasted Onion Soup with Croutons

1 Preheat oven to 250°. Remove root, tough outer leaves, and tops from leeks. Cut in half lengthwise. Slice leeks; rinse well, and drain. Combine leeks and next 4 ingredients on a large rimmed baking sheet, tossing to coat with oil. Sprinkle onion mixture with 1 tsp. salt and ½ tsp. pepper. Bake, uncovered, at 250° for 1 hour, stirring every 15 minutes.

2 Cook bacon in a Dutch oven until crisp; drain, reserving bacon and 1 Tbsp. drippings in pan. Add onion mixture to bacon mixture. Add broth. Bring to a boil; reduce heat, cover, and simmer 30 minutes or until onions are soft. Remove from heat, and let cool slightly.

3 Process soup, in batches, in a blender until smooth. Pour each batch of pureed soup into a bowl. Return soup to pan; stir in cream, ½ tsp. salt, and remaining ½ tsp. pepper. Keep warm.

4 Preheat oven to 350°. Place bread cubes in a large bowl. Drizzle bread cubes with butter, and sprinkle with remaining ½ tsp. salt; toss well. Spread bread cubes in a single layer on a large baking sheet. Bake at 350° for 12 minutes or until crisp, turning with a wide spatula after 6 minutes.

5 Ladle soup into bowls, and sprinkle with croutons. Serve immediately.
6 servings

Leeks, 2 medium
White onions, 2 large thinly sliced
Red onion, 1 small sliced
Garlic, 2 cloves minced
Olive oil, 3 Tbsp.
Kosher salt, 2 tsp., divided
Freshly ground black pepper, 1 tsp., divided
Thick-cut smoked bacon, 5 slices chopped
Chicken broth, 4 cups
Whipping cream, ½ cup
Rustic French bread, 2 cups ½-inch cubes
Unsalted butter, ¼ cup melted

Drink: English Porter Ale

"I love a big assortment of veggies in my minestrone, but use what you have, provided it's fresh and in season. The ricotta crostini are delicious solo or floating atop this filling meal in a bowl."

Carrots, 1 cup diced
Onion, 1 cup chopped
Celery, 1 cup chopped
Olive oil, ¼ cup
Pancetta, 4 oz. finely diced
Chicken stock, 8 cups
Fresh Italian parsley, 3 Tbsp. chopped
Fresh rosemary, 1 tsp. chopped
Shelled fava beans, 2 cups cooked and peeled
Fresh English peas, 2 cups
Fresh spinach, 1 cup loosely packed chopped
Chickpeas, 2 (16-oz.) cans drained and rinsed
Kosher salt, ½ tsp.
Freshly ground black pepper, ½ tsp.
Parmigiano-Reggiano cheese, ½ cup freshly grated
Herbed Ricotta Crostini

carrots + celery + pancetta + rosemary

Fava Bean Minestrone

1 Sauté first 3 ingredients in a stockpot in olive oil over medium heat 8 minutes or until tender. Add pancetta; sauté 7 minutes or until crisp. Add chicken stock and next 2 ingredients. Bring to a boil; reduce heat, and simmer, uncovered, 20 minutes. Add fava beans and next 5 ingredients. Return to a boil; reduce heat, and simmer, uncovered, 8 to 10 minutes or until vegetables are tender, stirring occasionally.

2 Ladle soup into bowls; sprinkle with Parmigiano-Reggiano cheese, and serve with Herbed Ricotta Crostini. 6 servings

herbed ricotta crostini:

Ricotta cheese, 1 cup
Fresh parsley, 1 Tbsp. chopped
Fresh basil, 1 Tbsp. chopped
Parmigiano-Reggiano cheese, 1 Tbsp. freshly grated

Kosher salt, ¼ tsp.
Freshly ground black pepper, ¼ tsp.
Country bread slices, 12
Olive oil, 3 Tbsp.

1 Heat a grill pan over medium-high heat. Stir together first 6 ingredients in a medium bowl until blended. Brush bread slices with olive oil; sprinkle with salt and pepper to taste.

2 Place bread slices on grill pan, and grill 1 to 2 minutes on each side or until toasted. Spoon 1 heaping Tbsp. cheese mixture onto each bread slice. 6 servings

Drink: French Grenache

"Serve this as a first course at your next holiday meal. I love the distinctive flavor of the chestnuts, and apple cider and Marsala pair beautifully with them. This is one of the few times you'll see me use cream in this book. It's worth the splurge. Steamed and peeled chestnuts are fall and winter harvests, and they're hard to track down during other times of year. Williams-Sonoma starts carrying them before Thanksgiving, and they sell out before the big day, so stock up and buy a few jars so you can make this soup more than once a year."

apple cider   +   Marsala   +   cream   +   chestnuts

Sweet Marsala Chestnut Soup with Mascarpone

1 Bring apple cider to a boil in a medium saucepan; add onion. Bring to a boil; boil 3 minutes. Add Marsala. Bring to a boil; boil 8 minutes or until liquid almost evaporates. Stir in cream; reduce heat to medium, and cook 15 minutes or until mixture is reduced by half and is caramel colored.

2 Add broth and next 3 ingredients. Bring to a boil; reduce heat, and simmer 2 minutes. Remove from heat, and let cool slightly.

3 Process soup, in batches, in a blender until smooth. Ladle soup into bowls, and garnish, if desired. 6 servings

Drink: American Maple or Pumpkin Ale

Apple cider, 2 cups
Red onion, 1½ cups sliced
Sweet Marsala, ⅔ cup
Heavy cream, 1 cup
Chicken broth, 1 (32-oz.) carton
Roasted chestnuts, 1¾ cups sliced
Kosher salt, 2¼ tsp.
Freshly ground black pepper, 1 tsp.
Garnish: mascarpone cheese

"This salad is wildly popular in the Middle East. The ingredients are all important, but my Za'atar Spice Blend (page 21) with its oregano, thyme, sesame seeds, and ground sumac is key. If you don't want to make your own, visit worldspice.com to order their za'atar. They can make spice blends for you, too.

My restaurant recipe calls for purslane, often considered a pervasive weed because it literally grows in the cracks of sidewalks. Look for it in organic and specialty markets. Watercress is a worthy substitute."

Za'atar Spice Blend + *watercress* + *tomatoes* + *feta*

Fettoush

Pita rounds, 2
Olive oil, ⅓ cup plus 3 Tbsp., divided
Za'atar Spice Blend (page 21), 2 Tbsp.
Fresh lemon juice, 1½ Tbsp.
Kosher salt, 1 tsp.
Freshly ground black pepper, ½ tsp.
Watercress, 5 cups loosely packed
Feta cheese, ⅓ cup crumbled
Tomatoes, 2 lb. cut into ½-inch pieces (6 cups)
Red onion, 1 cut into paper-thin slices

1 Preheat oven to 400°. Stack pita rounds, and cut into 6 wedges. Divide wedges in half, and place in a large bowl. Drizzle 3 Tbsp. olive oil over wedges, and sprinkle with Za'atar Spice Blend; toss well. Spread pita wedges on a large rimmed baking sheet.

2 Bake at 400° for 10 minutes or until browned. Cool completely.

3 Whisk together remaining ⅓ cup olive oil, lemon juice, salt, and pepper in a large bowl. Add watercress and next 3 ingredients. Crumble pita chips over salad, and serve immediately. 6 servings

Drink: Limbic Ale

"Caprese salad is popular for good reason—it's a classic combination of ingredients that seem destined to be together."

tomatoes + fresh mozzarella + basil + red onion

Heirloom tomatoes, 4 medium cut into
    ½-inch-thick slices
Fresh mozzarella cheese, 2 (8-oz.) balls
    cut into ½-inch-thick slices
Pickled Onions, 1 cup
Basil Oil, ½ cup
White balsamic vinegar, ½ cup
Fresh basil leaves, 12 torn into small pieces

Pickled Onions
Red onion, 1 thinly sliced
Cider vinegar, ½ cup
Kosher salt, ½ tsp.

Basil Oil
Fresh basil leaves, ½ cup packed
Garlic, 1 small clove coarsely chopped
Vegetable oil, 6 Tbsp.
Olive oil, 2 Tbsp.
Kosher salt, ½ tsp.
Freshly ground black pepper, ¼ tsp.

Todd's Insalata Caprese

❶ Arrange tomato and cheese slices alternately in a circular pattern on a serving plate. Top with Pickled Onions. Drizzle with Basil Oil and vinegar, and sprinkle with basil. 8 servings

Note: If you don't have time to make the Basil Oil or the Pickled Onions, try drizzling a little basil pesto over the tomatoes instead for a punch of flavor.

pickled onions:

❶ Bring 4 cups water to a boil in a 2-qt. saucepan. Add onion slices, and cook 1 minute; drain. Return onion to pan; add vinegar, salt, and ½ cup water. Bring to a boil; reduce heat and simmer, uncovered, 1 minute. Cool completely. Cover and store in the refrigerator up to 1 week. 2 cups

basil oil:

❶ Process basil and garlic in a blender until chopped. Add oils, salt, and pepper; process until smooth. ½ cup

drink: Olives' Rosé Sangria (page 41)

"This salad is a match made in heaven for lamb, because the bright citrus and distinctive anise flavor of the fennel balance the richness of the meat."

orange + parsley + lemon juice + fennel

Orange Fennel Salad

Navel oranges, 4
Fresh parsley, ½ cup chopped
Extra virgin olive oil, ¼ cup
Fresh lemon juice, 2 Tbsp.
Kosher salt, ½ tsp.
Freshly ground black pepper, ½ tsp.
Fennel bulbs, 2 large thinly sliced
Garnish: fennel fronds

Drink: Unoaked California Chardonnay

1 Section oranges over a bowl, squeezing pith to extract ¼ cup juice. Add parsley and next 5 ingredients; toss gently. Garnish, if desired. 7 servings

Cut a thin slice off the top and bottom of the orange; then stand it upright. Slice off the peel, pith, and membrane in thick strips following the contours of the fruit. Hold the fruit over a bowl; cut along each side of the membrane between the sections, letting each segment drop into the bowl as it's sliced.

"In Asia, pomelos are abundant and commonly used in cooking when citrus is required. I often use grapefruit, too. No matter what citrus you choose, you won't believe how the ingredients combine to create the perfect balance of sweet, salty, and sour. The dressing alone is amazing. If you can't find the dried Thai chiles, substitute red pepper flakes for some heat."

Fresh lime juice, ⅓ cup (about 2 limes)
Coconut water or coconut milk, ¼ cup
Canola oil, ¼ cup
Fish sauce, 4 tsp.
Dried Thai chiles, ½ tsp. minced (about 3 chiles)
Jumbo lump crabmeat, 1 lb. drained
Fresh cilantro leaves, ½ cup chopped
Red grapefruit, 3 sectioned

lime juice + *fish sauce* + *Thai chiles* + *cilantro*

Grapefruit and Crab Salad

1 Whisk together first 5 ingredients; cover and chill 20 minutes.

2 Pick crabmeat, removing any bits of shell. Combine crabmeat, cilantro, and dressing; toss well. Add grapefruit sections; toss gently. 6 servings

Drink: New Zealand Sauvignon Blanc

sherry vinegar   +   *Dijon mustard*   +   *Roquefort*   +   *walnuts*

Endive and Watercress Salad

1 Prepare vinaigrette: Whisk together all ingredients in a small bowl. Cover and chill.

2 Prepare salad: Remove and discard tough stems from watercress. Wash thoroughly, and drain. Cut watercress into 2-inch pieces and place in a large bowl. Add chopped endive, parsley, and 6 Tbsp. vinaigrette; toss well. Sprinkle cheese and walnuts over salad just before serving over endive spears. 8 servings

Drink: French Viognier

"Sharp Roquefort and crunchy walnuts pair beautifully with the bitter greens. If you would like, you can use my Basic Vinaigrette (page 16) and feel free to improvise from there. Vinaigrettes are how the French make any salad taste good!"

Vinaigrette
Extra virgin olive oil, ½ cup
Sherry vinegar, ¼ cup
Dijon mustard, 1 Tbsp.
Shallots, 2 tsp. minced
Kosher salt, ½ tsp.
Freshly ground black pepper, ¼ tsp.

Salad
Watercress, 1½ bunches
Belgian endive, 2 heads chopped and 2 heads whole
Fresh parsley, 2 Tbsp. chopped
Roquefort cheese, 2 oz. crumbled
Walnuts, 3 Tbsp. chopped and toasted

"Here's another simple but elegant salad that brings together ingredients with a natural affinity for each other. Stacking this salad is easy, but somehow guests believe you are a creative genius simply by doing so—let them think so, because you are. I like to use frisée or curly endive for this salad. Regular endive will work, too, if you cut it crosswise into thin rings."

blue cheese   curly endive   tomatoes   walnuts

Brandywine Tomato Stacks

Italian bread, 12 (¼-inch-thick) slices halved crosswise

Extra virgin olive oil, 6 Tbsp., divided

Fine sea salt, ½ tsp., divided

Freshly ground black pepper, ½ tsp., divided

Fresh lemon juice, 2 tsp.

Curly endive, 1 large head torn

Walnuts, 1½ cups coarsely chopped and toasted

Blue cheese, 6 oz. crumbled

Brandywine (or other heirloom) tomatoes, 4 (4-inch) cut into ¼-inch-thick slices

❶ Preheat oven to 350°. Place bread slices on a large rimmed baking sheet. Brush both sides of bread slices with ¼ cup olive oil; sprinkle with ¼ tsp. salt and ¼ tsp. pepper. Bake at 350° for 5 minutes or until toasted. Turn bread over; bake 5 more minutes or until toasted. Cool on wire racks.

❷ Combine remaining 2 Tbsp. olive oil, lemon juice, and remaining ¼ tsp. each salt and pepper in a large bowl. Add endive; toss well.

❸ Place a toast slice on a serving plate. Place 2 Tbsp. endive mixture on top of toast; sprinkle with 1 Tbsp. walnuts and 1 Tbsp. cheese. Top with a tomato slice.

❹ Repeat procedure with remaining toast slices, endive mixture, walnuts, cheese, and tomato slices. 12 servings

Drink: Washington Riesling

"This is a perfect interpretation of summertime. Ripe, freshly picked peaches are key. If you can't find them, watermelon makes a refreshing sub. And don't tell the Greeks, but I think Bulgarian feta sends this over the top. It's uncharacteristically creamy."

lemon   +   *feta*   +   *mint*

Peach-and-Fennel Salad with Feta and Mint

1 Grate zest from lemon to equal 2 tsp.; squeeze juice from lemon to equal 2 Tbsp. Whisk together zest, juice, 1 Tbsp. olive oil, ¼ tsp. salt, and ⅛ tsp. pepper in a small bowl.

2 Cut fennel into very thin slices using a mandoline or sharp knife. Stir together fennel, peaches, feta, mint, and remaining 1 Tbsp. olive oil in a large bowl. Add lemon mixture, and toss gently. Top with ½ tsp. freshly ground pepper just before serving. 8 servings

Watermelon-and-Fennel Salad with Feta and Mint: Substitute 3 cups cubed seedless watermelon for peaches. Proceed with recipe as directed.

Lemon, 1
Extra virgin olive oil, 2 Tbsp., divided
Kosher salt, ¼ tsp.
Freshly ground black pepper, ⅛ tsp.
Fennel bulbs, 2 medium
Peaches, 4 large ripe (about 1 lb.) sliced
Feta cheese, 1 cup crumbled
Fresh mint leaves, 4 large cut into thin strips
Freshly ground black pepper, ½ tsp.

Drink: Watermelon Cooler (page 40)

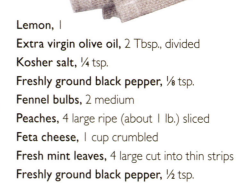

"Beets are a wonderful vegetable that tends to get a bad rap. But freshly roasted beets taste nothing like the canned, pickled version your mom might have made you eat as a kid. They're earthy, sweet, and have an incredible creamy texture. This recipe calls for a mix of beets, but as always, just buy the beets that look the best. If they still have their tops on them and the greens are crisp and bright, you know you're good to go."

beets + yellow onions + pistachios + goat cheese

Roasted Beet Salad with Goat Cheese and Pistachios

① Preheat oven to 400°. Rinse and scrub beets under cold running water; pat dry with paper towels. Trim stems and roots from beets, and place in a large bowl. Add onions. Drizzle vegetables with oil; sprinkle with salt and pepper, tossing to coat. Place vegetables on a large baking sheet. Cover tightly with aluminum foil.

② Bake at 400° for 1 hour and 30 minutes or until tender. Uncover vegetables, and let stand on baking sheet on a wire rack 15 minutes or until cool enough to handle.

③ Heat pistachios in a small nonstick skillet over medium-low heat, stirring often, 2 minutes or until lightly toasted and fragrant. Transfer to a plate to cool.

④ Peel beets. Cut beets into 1-inch cubes and onions into 1-inch pieces; place in a large bowl. Drizzle with 3 Tbsp. Orange-Mint Vinaigrette; toss to coat. Place lettuce in a separate large bowl. Drizzle with remaining 3 Tbsp. vinaigrette; toss well. Place 1⅓ cups lettuce mixture on each of 6 plates. Top each with about ¾ cup beet mixture. Sprinkle with pistachios and goat cheese. 8 servings

Golden beets, 1 lb.
Red beets, 1 lb.
Yellow onions, 2 quartered
Extra virgin olive oil, ¼ cup
Kosher salt, 1 tsp.
Freshly ground black pepper, ½ tsp.
Unsalted dry-roasted pistachios, ½ cup
Orange-Mint Vinaigrette (page 17),
    6 Tbsp., divided
Spring mix lettuce blend, 8 cups
Goat cheese, 3 oz. crumbled

Drink: Italian Chardonnay

"This is a clean, bright salad that feels decadent because of the dressing. No one needs to know that buttermilk and yogurt replace most of the fat in the dressing! (Knowing that, it's hard for me not to drink it!) For a larger meal, serve the salad with grilled chicken or shrimp over the top."

buttermilk + lime juice + garlic + jalapeño

Chopped Salad

Hearts of palm slices, ¼ cup
Pitted Spanish olive slices, 2 Tbsp.
Belgian endive, 4 heads cut into thin strips
Romaine hearts, 3
Radicchio, 1 head cut into thin strips
Plum tomato, 1 large finely diced
Lime-Jalapeño Ranch Dressing, 1¼ cups
Avocado, ½ cup finely diced
Kosher salt and freshly ground black
   pepper to taste
Country-style croutons, 1 cup

1 Combine first 6 ingredients in a large bowl. Drizzle with Lime-Jalapeño Ranch Dressing; toss well. Add avocado, salt, and pepper, and toss gently. Sprinkle with croutons, and serve immediately. 4 servings

lime-jalapeño ranch dressing:

Plain Greek yogurt, ½ cup
Buttermilk, ⅓ cup
Mayonnaise, 3 Tbsp.
Fresh lime juice, 1½ tsp.
Dijon mustard, 1 tsp.

Shallot, 1 thinly sliced
Garlic, 1 clove
Jalapeño pepper, 1 halved and seeded
Fresh chives, 1 Tbsp. finely chopped

1 Process all ingredients, except chives, in a blender until smooth. Transfer to a bowl; stir in chives. 1½ cups

Drink: Alsace Riesling

"This classic salad hails from the sunny seaside town of Nice, France. I've replaced the usual canned tuna with pan-seared tuna served rare. Cook the tuna over high heat for a beautiful crusty exterior. It's perfect lunch fare, or great as a light summer dinner, too."

Tuna Niçoise

1 Cook green beans in salted boiling water for 3 to 5 minutes, or just until tender; remove with slotted spoon. Plunge beans into ice water to stop the cooking process; drain. Cook potatoes in salted boiling water to cover 5 minutes or just until tender. Drain and cool completely. Chop potatoes.

2 Meanwhile, whisk together ½ tsp. salt, ¼ tsp. pepper, extra virgin olive oil, and next 2 ingredients in a bowl until blended. Whisk in shallots and garlic. Cover and chill.

3 Sprinkle tuna with remaining ¼ tsp. salt and ¼ tsp. pepper. Heat olive oil in a small skillet over high heat. Cook tuna in hot oil 1 minute on each side. Remove from pan; let stand 5 minutes.

4 Place green beans in a medium bowl; drizzle with 1 Tbsp. dressing, and toss to coat. Repeat procedure with potatoes and tomatoes in separate bowls.

5 Cut tuna into thin slices. Arrange tuna, green beans, potatoes, tomatoes, eggs, olives, and mixed greens on a serving platter. Serve with remaining dressing.
6 servings

Trimmed green beans, 1 (12-oz.) package
Baby red potatoes, 1 lb.
Kosher salt, ¾ tsp., divided
Freshly ground black pepper, ½ tsp., divided
Extra virgin olive oil, ⅓ cup
Orange zest, 1 Tbsp.
Fresh orange juice, ¼ cup
Shallots, 1 Tbsp. minced
Garlic, 1 small clove minced
Sushi-grade tuna loin, 1 lb.
Olive oil, 2 Tbsp.
Tomatoes, 1 cup diced
Large eggs, 4 hard-cooked quartered
Pitted oil-cured olives, ½ cup
Spring mix lettuce blend, 6 cups

Drink: French Chablis

"This salad combines some of my favorite ingredients in the world—buttery tuna, herbs and aromatics, and my favorite world flavors like harissa and za'atar—to create a luxurious salad that is hard to stop eating!"

parsley + harissa + green onions + mint

Tuna Tabbouleh with Harissa Vinaigrette

1 Place bulgur in a heatproof bowl. Bring vegetable stock to a boil; pour over bulgur. Cover bowl with foil, and let stand 1 hour.

2 Drain bulgur through a fine wire-mesh strainer, pressing bulgur against sides with a wooden spoon. Discard liquid. Return bulgur to bowl. Stir in parsley and next 5 ingredients. Add tuna, and toss gently. 8 servings

Bulgur wheat, 1 cup
Vegetable stock, 1½ cups
Fresh parsley, 1 cup finely chopped
Harissa Vinaigrette (page 17), ½ cup
Plum tomato, ¼ cup diced
Green onions, 2 Tbsp. diagonally cut thin slices
Fresh mint, 2 Tbsp. chopped
Kosher salt, ½ tsp.
Ahi tuna, 8 oz. uncooked sushi grade finely diced

Drink: California Pinot Rosé

Slice the tuna with long, sweeping strokes for smooth cuts. Stack a few slices on top of one another, and then halve lengthwise, and cut crosswise into a uniform dice.

tabbouleh (tuh-BOO-leh) n. A Middle Eastern dish of bulgur wheat, chopped tomatoes, and onions, traditionally flavored with parsley, mint, olive oil, and lemon juice.

"Make the batter in the morning, then cook the falafel up quickly before dinner. Grill the corn if you have a chance; it adds yet another dimension of flavor. Raita is the perfect condiment, but if you're short on time just top these with a dollop of plain yogurt or drizzle of tahini that has been thinned with a splash of lemon juice and water."

chickpeas   corn   cumin   parsley

Corn Falafel

1 To prepare falafel, rinse chickpeas; drain.

2 With processor running, drop garlic cloves, 1 at a time, through food chute. Process until minced. Add onion, chickpeas, corn, and next 5 ingredients; process until mixture resembles mashed peas. Sprinkle flour and baking powder over chickpea mixture. Pulse 10 times or until blended. Transfer to a bowl; cover and refrigerate 3 hours or until thoroughly chilled.

3 To prepare raita, stir together all ingredients in a bowl. Cover and chill until ready to serve.

4 Pour oil to a depth of 1½ inches into a large heavy skillet. Heat to 350°.

5 Meanwhile, shape chickpea mixture into 48 (1-inch) balls. Fry balls, in batches, in hot oil 1 minute or until golden and crisp. Drain on paper towels. Place 6 falafel on half of each naan. Spoon about ½ cup raita over falafel; fold in half. Serve immediately. 8 servings

Drink: Irish Red Ale

Falafel
Chickpeas (garbanzo beans), 1 can
Garlic, 4 cloves
Onion, 1 cup chopped
Fresh corn kernels, 1 cup (2 ears)
Fresh parsley, 2 Tbsp. chopped
Fresh cilantro, 2 Tbsp. chopped
Kosher salt, 1 tsp.
Ground cumin, 1 tsp.
Crushed red pepper, ½ tsp.
All-purpose flour, 6 Tbsp.
Baking powder, 1 tsp.

Raita
Plain Greek yogurt, 2 cups
Fresh mint, ¼ cup chopped
Ground cumin, 2 tsp.
Kosher salt, ¼ tsp.
Freshly ground black pepper, ¼ tsp.
Ground red pepper, ⅛ tsp.
Cucumbers, 2 peeled and diced (2 cups)

Remaining Ingredients
Canola oil
Naan, 8 warmed

"Shawarma is a 'fast food' you'll find in the Mediterranean, Middle East, and even Australia. Each region has its own version of thinly sliced, grilled or spit-roasted meat that comes wrapped in flat bread.

I use butterflied chicken breasts dusted in my Shawarma Spice Blend (page 20) because they cook in a mere 5 minutes. Serve the chicken in store-bought pita bread or naan with all the toppings, and you've got a meal that tastes out of this world on the table in minutes."

Skinned and boned chicken breasts, 2
    (about 1¼ lb.))
Shawarma Spice Blend (page 20), 2 tsp.
Kosher salt, ½ tsp.
Freshly ground black pepper, ½ tsp.
Olive oil, 2 Tbsp.
Plain Greek yogurt, 3 Tbsp.
Tahini, 1 Tbsp.
Sriracha sauce, 1 tsp.
Curry Aioli (page 23), ¼ cup
Naan, 4 warmed
Toppings: thin red onion slices, tomato slices,
    chopped romaine lettuce

Drink: Chilean Sauvignon Gris or
    Sauvignon Blanc

Shawarma Spice Blend   +   tahini   +   sriracha sauce   +   Curry Aioli

Chicken Shawarma Sandwiches

1 Butterfly chicken breasts by making a lengthwise cut in 1 side, cutting to but not through the opposite side; unfold. Place between 2 sheets of heavy-duty plastic wrap, and flatten to ½-inch thickness, using a rolling pin or the flat side of a meat mallet. Sprinkle both sides of chicken with Shawarma Spice Blend, salt, and pepper.

2 Heat olive oil in a large skillet over medium heat. Cook chicken in hot oil 3 minutes on each side. Remove from pan; let stand 5 minutes. Cut chicken diagonally into ½-inch strips.

3 Stir together yogurt, tahini, and sriracha sauce in a small bowl.

4 Spread 1 Tbsp. yogurt mixture and 1 Tbsp. Curry Aioli on each naan. Layer chicken strips, onion slices, tomato slices, and lettuce over aioli; fold up. 4 servings

Variation: Use ¼ recipe of either of my pizza doughs (page 34) as the bread for this recipe. Simply shape a piece of dough into a 10-inch round, then heat 1 Tbsp. olive oil in a frying pan over medium heat. Cook the dough for 3 minutes per side, or until it is just cooked through and browned. It's the perfect base for this sandwich!

"Let the lobster rule—I should have a t-shirt with that on the front. Truly, it's such a standout ingredient that it doesn't need much. Beurre noisette, or brown butter, is a great complement to seafood. Make sure you use soft, warm bread. Potato rolls work great, or regular hot dog buns if they're fresh from a bakery. To extract the tail meat, press down on the top side of the tail shell firmly with both hands to crack, then flip the tail over and pull the soft underside of the shell apart. The meat comes out easily."

Unsalted butter, ¾ cup
Lobsters, 4 (1¼- to 1½-lb.) cooked
Mayonnaise, ⅓ cup
Fresh chives, ¼ cup chopped
Fresh parsley, 3 Tbsp. chopped
Hot dog buns, 4
Kosher salt and freshly
　ground black pepper
　to taste

Drink: Italian
　　　 Soave

Buttered Lobster Roll

1 Melt butter in a small saucepan over medium heat; cook 2 to 3 minutes or just until butter browns and develops a nutty aroma, skimming foam. (Do not overcook.) Remove from heat.

2 Twist legs and claws from bodies of lobsters. Separate tails from the abdomens. Cut shell of lobster tail segments lengthwise on top and underside using kitchen shears. Pry open tail segments; remove meat, and coarsely chop. Cut shell of claws and leg segments; pry open and remove meat. Coarsely chop meat. Discard shell.

3 Combine lobster meat, mayonnaise, chives, and parsley in a medium bowl. Fold in ½ cup browned butter.

4 Open buns, but do not separate halves. Brush remaining ¼ cup browned butter over cut sides of buns. Place buns, cut sides down, in a skillet over high heat, and toast until lightly browned.

5 Spoon about 1 cup lobster mixture into each bun. Add salt and pepper to taste. Serve immediately. 4 servings

Grab the knuckle and pull backward to separate it from the claw.

Remove the meat from the knuckle with the tip of an oyster knife.

Repeat the same technique for the other knuckle and claw.

Slice through the center of the claw's shell without slicing through the meat using a knife or lobster crackers. (This can dull your knife, but it sure works well!)

Separate half of the shell from the claw.

Expose the claw meat inside.

Wiggle the pincer claw to loosen the meat.

Repeat with the other claw.

Ta da! The claw and knuckle meat are removed.

"Oh my gosh, I love eggs. I'll put them on anything—steaks, salads, pasta—and whip them up numerous ways for brunch. I truly appreciate the simplicity of this egg salad. The addition of bacon gives it a breakfast-for-lunch vibe. Choose a delicious multigrain or homemade wheat bread and toast it for extra crunch."

Dijon mustard + *red wine vinegar* + *black pepper* + *celery*

Bacon and Egg Salad Sandwiches

1 Stir together first 5 ingredients in a medium bowl. Stir in onion and celery. Add eggs and bacon; stir gently.

2 Spread toast slices with mayonnaise and Dijon mustard. Top each of 5 toast slices with about ¾ cup egg salad, a lettuce leaf, and another toast slice. 5 servings

Drink: Spicy Bloody Mary or beer

Mayonnaise, 1 cup
Dijon mustard, 2 Tbsp.
Red wine vinegar, 1 Tbsp.
Kosher salt, ½ tsp.
Freshly ground black pepper, ¼ tsp.
Red onion, ½ cup finely diced
Celery ribs, 6 finely diced
Large eggs, 10 hard-cooked, peeled, and chopped
Bacon slices, 4 thick cooked coarsely chopped
Whole wheat bread, 10 slices toasted
Mayonnaise
Dijon mustard
Romaine lettuce, 5 large leaves

sauerkraut + *Swiss cheese* + *caraway seeds* + *celery leaves*

Pastrami Flatbread "Sandwiches"

❶ Preheat oven to 400°. If using a pizza stone, place in oven to preheat.

❷ Sprinkle flour on a large, flat surface or cutting board. Divide dough into 4 (4-oz.) rounds. Roll each round into a 10-inch circle, sprinkling surface with flour as needed to prevent sticking.

❸ Place dough circles on a preheated pizza stone or 2 lightly floured baking sheets. Top with sauerkraut, cheese, and caraway seeds. Drizzle with desired amount of olive oil, and sprinkle with salt and pepper.

❹ Bake at 400° for 5 minutes. Top with pastrami, and bake 5 more minutes or until cheese is melted and dough is lightly browned and done. Remove from oven. Sprinkle with celery leaves, if desired, and drizzle with mustard. 4 servings

Drink:
French Saison/Farmhouse Ale

"I use the term 'flatbread' loosely for this recipe, because most people want to fold it up and try to fit the whole thing in their mouth like a sandwich. It's just that good. Try one of my pizza dough recipes as the base (page 34), or purchase one of the high-quality pre-made doughs that are so readily available."

All-purpose flour
Pizza dough, 1 lb. homemade (page 34) or bakery
Sauerkraut, 1 cup canned drained
Swiss cheese, 1 cup (4 oz.) freshly grated
Caraway seeds, 1 tsp.
Extra virgin olive oil
Kosher salt
Freshly ground black pepper
Pastrami, ¼ lb. thinly sliced
Celery leaves, ¼ cup (optional)
Yellow mustard, 2 Tbsp.

"My favorite sandwich on the planet. Seriously. It's crunchy, creamy, salty, tangy…pretty much perfection on a plate. Use leftover Slow-Roasted Pork (page 183) as the base of this masterpiece."

Spicy Aioli + *Swiss cheese* + *Dill pickles* + *butter*

Cuban Reuben

French bread baguette, 1 (8-oz.)
Rice vinegar, 2 Tbsp.
Spicy Aioli (page 23)
Swiss cheese, 8 slices
Slow-Roasted Pork (page 183), 12 oz.
Ham, 12 thin slices (8 oz.)
Dill pickles, 2 thinly sliced lengthwise
Unsalted butter, 2 Tbsp. melted

Drink: French Merlot-based blend or plain Merlot

❶ Preheat a panini press. Cut baguette crosswise into 4 pieces; cut each piece in half horizontally. Stir vinegar into Spicy Aioli. Spread cut sides of bread with mixture. Layer cheese, Slow-Roasted Pork, ham slices, and pickle slices on bottoms of baguette pieces; top with baguette tops. Brush outsides of sandwiches with melted butter.

❷ Cook sandwiches, 2 at a time, in panini press 5 minutes or until cheese melts and sandwiches are thoroughly heated. 4 servings

panini (pah-NEE-nee) n. derived from the Italian panino or sandwich, now commonly refers to a grilled pressed sandwich.

Vegetables

If I can encourage you to do one thing, it's to learn to shop seasonally for produce. We have become so accustomed to seeing vegetables available year-round that many of us don't remember or will never understand that garden ingredients have seasons in which they thrive. Asparagus should be enjoyed with gusto in spring and bidden farewell after a few months. Understanding this agricultural clock allows you to anticipate and celebrate a vegetable when it arrives and move on to what's next when the time comes. That will ensure an interesting and varied diet.

When looking for the best produce, try to buy things as whole as possible—carrots with their tops on and tomatoes on the vine. The freshness of the attached greens signals whether the produce has just been harvested or has sat around for days. Smell your produce. Look for vivid color. Start there, and you'll be amazed at how little fuss these vegetables need to be enjoyed.

"I'm a huge broccoli nut. My mother never had to tell me to eat my broccoli growing up! This recipe is delicious as a side or as a main dish when served over *quadrucci,* one of my favorite little square pastas. For an Asian twist, trade the lemon juice and olive oil for a little soy sauce and sesame oil, and serve with brown rice."

Fresh broccoli, 1 lb. cut into 1-inch pieces
Extra virgin olive oil, 3 Tbsp.
Garlic, 2 cloves thinly sliced
Crushed red pepper, ¼ tsp.
Lemon zest, 2 tsp.
Fresh lemon juice, 1 Tbsp.
Fine, dry breadcrumbs, 2 tsp.
Kosher salt, ¼ tsp.
Freshly ground black pepper, ⅛ tsp.

olive oil   +   garlic   +   red pepper   +   lemon zest

Spicy Broccoli Salad

❶ Sauté broccoli in hot olive oil in a large skillet over medium-high heat for 5 minutes or until lightly browned. Add garlic slices and crushed red pepper; sauté 1 minute or until garlic is toasted. Transfer broccoli mixture to a bowl. Add lemon zest, lemon juice, and remaining ingredients; toss well. 4 servings

"Like Brussels sprouts, cauliflower gets a bad rap. That's because most people don't know the ideal way to cook it. By searing it in a pan or roasting it with very high heat in an oven, cauliflower caramelizes, becomes sweet yet holds its shape…unlike the mushiness that steaming often produces. Flavored with cinnamon and raisins, this is a beautiful side dish or fulfilling vegetarian main course with exotic flavors."

 + +  +

golden raisins *shallot* *cinnamon* *arugula*

Fire-Roasted Cauliflower

1 Combine raisins and 1 cup warm water in a bowl; let stand 1 hour. Drain, reserving 2 Tbsp. raisin liquid.

2 Preheat oven to 500°. Place cauliflower in a large bowl. Add carrot, 2 Tbsp. oil, ½ tsp. salt, and ¼ tsp. pepper; toss well. Spread cauliflower mixture in a single layer on a large baking sheet. Bake at 500° for 12 minutes or until vegetables are crisp-tender. Place vegetables in a large bowl.

3 Meanwhile, process reserved raisin liquid, remaining ¼ cup olive oil, remaining ¼ tsp. salt and ¼ tsp. pepper, shallot, and cinnamon in a blender until shallot is finely minced. Pour shallot mixture over vegetable mixture; add raisins, and toss to coat. Serve over arugula. 8 servings

Golden raisins, ½ cup
Warm water (100° to 110°), 1 cup
Cauliflower, 2 cups cut into ½-inch florets
Carrots, 2 diagonally sliced into ½-inch pieces
Olive oil, 6 Tbsp. divided
Kosher salt, ¾ tsp., divided
Freshly ground black pepper, ½ tsp., divided
Shallot, 1 small halved
Ground cinnamon, ¼ tsp.
Baby arugula, 4 cups loosely packed

Mexican Corn Two Ways

Mayonnaise, ½ cup

Jalapeño pepper, 1 small seeded and minced

Feta cheese, 1 cup crumbled

Fresh corn, 6 ears husks removed

"Twenty years ago I tasted grilled corn from a street vendor in the Mission District of San Francisco. Ever since then, I've been noodling around with different preparations of corn on the cob. For a recipe like this, make sure you buy freshly harvested corn. The longer it sits, the more time the natural sugars in the corn have had to turn to starch. But, I'll admit, I've craved this in the off-season, and it still tasted pretty great prepared this way!"

Jalapeño-Feta Corn

1 Preheat grill to 350° to 400° (medium-high) heat. Stir together mayonnaise and jalapeño pepper in a small bowl. Place cheese on a shallow plate.

2 Grill corn, covered with grill lid, 20 minutes or until done, turning every 4 to 5 minutes. Generously spread corn with mayonnaise mixture. Roll corn in cheese. Serve immediately. 6 servings

Spicy Mint Mayo Variation: Combine mayonnaise with 2 Tbsp. chopped fresh mint and minced jalapeño pepper. Spread mint mayonnaise over grilled corn, and roll in crumbled feta cheese.

Wearing gloves when seeding hot peppers is a great way to keep you from accidentally rubbing some of the oils on your face.

"Corn is a great vehicle for bold flavors. Here, curry adds brightness to the sweetness of corn—it's a Far East spin on an ingredient we often cook the same way over and over."

Anaheim chiles + ginger + curry powder + coconut milk

Yellow Corn Curry

1 Hold each corn cob upright in a bowl, and carefully cut downward, cutting kernels from cob. Scrape milk and remaining pulp from cobs into a bowl; reserve cobs.

2 Heat 1 Tbsp. oil in a medium saucepan over medium heat. Add corn kernels, cobs, salt, and next 3 ingredients. Cook, stirring constantly, 4 minutes. Stir in curry powder; cook, uncovered, stirring occasionally, 2 minutes. Reduce heat to medium low. Add corn pulp mixture and coconut milk to corn kernel mixture. Cook, uncovered, 25 minutes or until corn is tender. Remove cobs and ginger.

3 Sauté onion, jalapeño pepper, and tomato in remaining 1 Tbsp. oil in a large skillet over medium-high heat 7 minutes or until onion is tender. Stir in corn mixture. Cook, uncovered, stirring occasionally, 15 minutes. 4 servings

Fresh corn, 2 ears husks removed

Canola oil, 2 Tbsp., divided

Kosher salt, 1 tsp.

Anaheim chiles, 2 halved and seeded

Garlic, 1 clove

Fresh ginger, 1 (1-inch) piece peeled

Curry powder, 1 Tbsp.

Coconut milk, 1 (13.5-oz.) can

Red onion, 1 sliced

Red jalapeño peppers, 2 seeded and cut into thin strips

Plum tomatoes, 4 diced

"Caution: This is ridiculously delicious, easy to make, and freezes well. Plus it's versatile…use it as the filling for my Sweet Corn Ravioli (page 132). Just make sure to use the freshest, sweetest corn possible to extract the most juice from the kernels."

onion + garlic + cream + butter

Creamed Corn

❶ Hold each corn cob upright in a bowl, and carefully cut downward, cutting kernels from cob; scrape milk and remaining pulp from cobs into bowl.

❷ Sauté onion and garlic in hot oil in a 3-qt. saucepan over medium heat 6 minutes or until tender. Add corn and salt. Cook, stirring often, 2 minutes; add cream. Bring to a boil; reduce heat, and simmer, stirring often, 20 minutes or until mixture is reduced to 4½ cups. Add butter, stirring until melted.

❸ Process 2½ cups corn mixture in a blender 1 minute or until smooth. Stir corn puree into remaining corn mixture in pan. Stir in pepper. 6 servings

Fresh corn, 6 ears husks removed
Onion, 1 small finely diced (about 1 cup)
Garlic, 1 clove minced
Canola oil, 2 Tbsp.
Kosher salt, 1½ tsp.
Heavy cream, 2 cups
Unsalted butter, ½ cup cut up
Freshly ground black pepper, ⅛ tsp.

Hold corn upright in a bowl and cut tips of kernels off with a chef's knife.
Scrape the cob with the backside of the knife to extract the sweet, milky juices from the corn into the bowl.

"I'm constantly looking for ways to use vegetable and fruit juices in my cooking. They add so much extra flavor without extra fat. Combined with a little ginger and honey, these carrots are unlike any you've ever tasted. You can juice your own carrots, or buy one of the many carrot juices sold in grocery stores these days."

carrot juice + honey + ground ginger + cinnamon

Roasted Carrots in Carrot Juice

Carrot juice, 1 cup
Chicken broth, 1 cup
Honey, ⅓ cup
Ground ginger, 1 tsp.
Cinnamon sticks, 2 (3-inch)
Carrots, 5 cups 1-inch pieces (about 2 lb.)
Olive oil, 2 Tbsp.
Fresh rosemary, 1 Tbsp.
Kosher salt, ½ tsp.
Freshly ground black pepper, ¼ tsp.
Unsalted butter, 1 Tbsp.

① Preheat oven to 500°. Bring first 5 ingredients to a boil in a medium saucepan; reduce heat to medium, and cook, uncovered, stirring occasionally, 30 minutes or until reduced to ⅔ cup. Remove from heat.

② Meanwhile, toss together carrots and next 4 ingredients in a large bowl. Spread carrot mixture on a large baking sheet. Bake at 500° for 20 minutes or until carrots are tender and beginning to brown, stirring twice. Place carrot mixture in a large bowl.

③ Remove cinnamon sticks from syrup. Bring syrup to a simmer over medium heat; add butter, stirring until melted. Pour over carrot mixture; toss to coat. Taste and adjust seasonings. 6 servings

"Carrots and parsnips should just go ahead and get married already. They are such a perfect match, and creamy, tart feta balances the sweetness of the vegetables. This is so easy, but such a great change-up from regular roasted veggies."

cumin   +   cilantro   +   garlic   +   feta

Roasted Carrots and Parsnips

1 Preheat oven to 400°. Place first 8 ingredients in a large bowl; toss well. Spread vegetable mixture onto a large ungreased baking sheet. Bake at 400° for 45 minutes or until tender and brown, stirring after 25 minutes. Place vegetables in a bowl, sprinkle with cheese, and garnish, if desired. 8 servings

Carrots, 1½ lb. peeled
   and cut into large chunks
Parsnips, 1½ lb. peeled and cut
   into 2-inch chunks
Ground cumin, 2 Tbsp.
Kosher salt, 2 tsp.
Freshly ground black pepper, 1 tsp.
Fresh cilantro, ¼ cup chopped
Garlic, 3 cloves finely chopped
Olive oil, 2 Tbsp.
Feta cheese, ½ cup crumbled
Garnish: fresh cilantro leaves

"With just a few ingredients, this side dish comes together quickly. I love to pair the beans with my Chicken Under a Brick (page 144) and my Creamy Miso Sweet Potatoes (page 112). One important step to note: After washing your green beans, dry them really well between paper towels. Any water on them will splatter when it hits the hot oil."

dark sesame oil + *black sesame seeds* + *white sesame seeds*

Black and White Sesame Green Beans

Dark sesame oil, 2 Tbsp.
Fresh green beans, 1 lb. trimmed
White sesame seeds, 1 Tbsp.
Black sesame seeds, 1 Tbsp.
Kosher salt, ½ tsp.
Freshly ground black pepper, ½ tsp.

1 Heat oil in a large nonstick skillet over medium-high heat. Sauté green beans 5 minutes or until almost tender. Sprinkle sesame seeds, salt, and pepper over beans; sauté 1 minute or until sesame seeds are toasted and beans are crisp-tender. 4 servings

"You're not going to believe how easy it is to give frozen peas new life. Mint and peas combine beautifully and taste like a mouthful of springtime. Either follow this recipe, or just cook the peas with a little of my compound butter with mint and shallots (page 19) to finish. Kids gobble these up!"

butter + mint + s&p

Pea Puree with Mint Butter

① Place peas in a wire-mesh strainer. Rinse under cold running water until thawed. Drain well.

② Melt butter in a large saucepan over medium heat. Add peas; sauté 3 minutes or until thoroughly heated. Process peas, mint, salt, and pepper in a blender until smooth. Garnish, if desired. 4 servings

Frozen petite peas, 1 (16-oz.) package
Unsalted butter, ¼ cup
Fresh mint, 2 Tbsp. coarsely chopped
Kosher salt, ½ tsp.
Freshly ground black pepper, ¼ tsp.
Garnish: fresh mint sprig

"Asparagus is another vegetable that begs to be roasted. The process brings out the robust, sweet flavors of this spring gem. Surprisingly, the bold flavors of asparagus and porcini mushrooms don't compete, but are earthy complements."

balsamic vinegar + lemon juice + garlic + Parmigiano-Reggiano

Roasted Asparagus Salad with Porcini Mushrooms

Dried porcini mushrooms, 1 (1-oz.) package
Hot water, 1 cup
Balsamic vinegar, ¼ cup
Fresh lemon juice, ¼ cup
Kosher salt, ¾ tsp., divided
Freshly ground black pepper, ½ tsp., divided
Garlic, 3 cloves chopped
Shallot, 1 small chopped
Extra virgin olive oil, ½ cup plus 1 Tbsp., divided
Fresh asparagus, 1 lb.
Parmigiano-Reggiano cheese, 1½ cups grated

❶ Combine mushrooms and 1 cup hot water. Let stand 30 minutes. Drain.

❷ Preheat oven to 400°. Combine balsamic vinegar, lemon juice, ½ tsp. salt, ¼ tsp. pepper, and next 2 ingredients in a small bowl. Gradually whisk in ½ cup olive oil.

❸ Snap off and discard tough ends of asparagus. Place asparagus in a large bowl. Drizzle asparagus with remaining 1 Tbsp. olive oil; sprinkle with remaining ¼ tsp. salt and remaining ¼ tsp. pepper, tossing to coat. Place in a single layer on a baking sheet. Bake at 400° for 10 minutes or until crisp-tender, basting once with vinaigrette and turning with tongs.

❹ Combine drained mushrooms and ¼ cup vinaigrette. Divide roasted asparagus among 4 plates. Drizzle each serving with about 3 Tbsp. vinaigrette. Spoon 3 Tbsp. mushroom mixture on top of each serving. Shave cheese over salads. 4 servings

Remove and discard the tough ends of asparagus spears before cooking. **Bend** each end until it snaps. It will snap where the tender part begins.

"You probably know what slow-roasting does to garlic, but have you ever thought about trying it with fennel? It concentrates the intrinsic sweetness of the bulb, making it a terrific accompaniment for stronger flavors. Try it next to my Grilled Maple-Brined Turkey (page 148) with a scoop of cranberry chutney, or slice some and fry it in a pan to crisp it up before making a salad of blood oranges and mixed greens dressed with my Basic Vinaigrette (page 16)."

olive oil   +   lemon   +   Parmigiano-Reggiano

Fennel, 3 bulbs (about 3 lb.)
Extra virgin olive oil, 3 Tbsp.
Kosher salt, 1 tsp.
Freshly ground black pepper, ½ tsp.
Lemon, 1 halved
Parmigiano-Reggiano cheese, ¾ cup shaved

Slow-Roasted Fennel

❶ Preheat oven to 250°. Rinse fennel thoroughly. Trim and discard root ends of fennel bulbs. Trim stalks from bulbs, reserving fronds for another use. Place fennel on a 15- x 12-inch piece of aluminum foil; drizzle with olive oil, and sprinkle with salt and pepper. Wrap foil tightly around fennel. Bake at 250° for 6 hours or until fennel is very tender. Let cool 5 minutes.

❷ Cut fennel into 1-inch pieces, and place in a bowl. Squeeze lemon halves over fennel, and sprinkle with cheese. 6 servings

sugar + olive oil + butter

Zucchini Pancakes

1 Whisk together flour, baking powder, sugar, and salt in a large bowl. Whisk together eggs and oil in a medium bowl; stir in zucchini. Add zucchini mixture to flour mixture, stirring just until dry ingredients are moistened.

2 Pour about ¼ cup batter for each pancake onto a hot, lightly greased griddle or large nonstick skillet. Cook pancakes 4 to 5 minutes or until tops are covered with bubbles and edges look dry and cooked; turn and cook other side. Transfer pancakes to a warm plate, spreading each with about ½ to 1 tsp. butter. Top with desired toppings. 4 servings

Note: Keep pancakes warm in a 200° oven, if necessary, for up to 30 minutes.

"I never tire of zucchini. Ever. This zucchini twist on the classic potato pancake is a great way to use up a bumper crop. Top the pancakes with almost anything—like my Roasted Tomatoes (page 30), My Favorite Pesto (page 28), or a little Greek yogurt thinned with lemon juice."

All-purpose flour, ¾ cup
Baking powder, 4 tsp.
Sugar, ½ tsp.
Kosher salt, ½ tsp.
Large eggs, 4
Extra virgin olive oil, 3 Tbsp.
Zucchini, 2 cups finely shredded and drained
Unsalted butter, 3 to 4 Tbsp. softened
Toppings: Greek yogurt, My Favorite Pesto
   (page 28), Roasted Tomatoes (page 30)

"Brussels sprouts are misunderstood—probably because most people don't know how to cook them properly. Roasted in the oven, they become sweet and caramelized—the perfect platform for other layers of flavor such as apples, onions, and smoky bacon. This recipe will convert folks to the Brussels sprout–loving team! The Chestnut Puree is unbelievable. Try it with my Grilled Maple-Brined Turkey (page 148), too."

Brussels sprouts, 2 lb.
Olive oil, 2 Tbsp.
Kosher salt, ½ tsp.
Freshly ground black pepper, ¼ tsp.
Thick bacon slices, 6 cut into ½-inch pieces
Gala apple, 1 peeled and chopped
  (about ¾ cup)
Onion, ½ medium thinly sliced
Lemon, ½ medium
Chestnut Puree (optional)

bacon + Gala apple + onion + lemon

Oven-Roasted Brussels Sprouts with Apples, Onions, and Crispy Bacon

1 Preheat oven to 450°. Remove discolored leaves from Brussels sprouts. Cut off stem ends, and cut a shallow X in the bottom of each sprout. Place Brussels sprouts in a large bowl. Drizzle with olive oil, salt, and pepper; toss to coat. Spread sprouts on a large baking sheet.

2 Bake at 450° for 20 minutes or until brown and tender, stirring after 10 minutes. Transfer sprouts to a large bowl.

3 Meanwhile, cook bacon in a large nonstick skillet over medium heat, stirring often, 5 to 6 minutes or until crisp. Remove bacon from skillet with a slotted spoon, and drain on paper towels, reserving 1 Tbsp. drippings in skillet.

4 Cook apple and onion in hot drippings over medium heat 10 to 12 minutes or until tender and beginning to brown. Pour apple and onion over Brussels sprouts. Squeeze lemon half over mixture, and sprinkle with bacon; toss gently.

5 Spoon each serving of Brussels sprouts over about 4 Tbsp. Chestnut Puree, if desired. 6 servings

Chestnut Puree: While this is available in most grocery stores, you can also make your own. Cook 1½ cups chestnut puree and ¾ cup milk in a medium saucepan over medium heat, stirring constantly, 6 to 8 minutes or until hot. Stir in 3 Tbsp. maple syrup and ⅛ tsp. each salt and pepper. Process mixture with a handheld blender until smooth. 2 cups

"Miso added to sweet potatoes introduces an uncommon depth of flavor that leaves people asking for more! Use a ricer or food mill to mash the potatoes into a silky puree. Serve this as the base for Chicken Under a Brick (page 144), Black and White Sesame Green Beans (page 104) or Oven-Roasted Brussels Sprouts with Apples, Onions, and Crispy Bacon (page 110). Miso is sold in the refrigerated section of most grocery stores. Try a tablespoon in your vinaigrette."

butter   +   miso   +   cream

Creamy Miso Sweet Potatoes

Sweet potatoes, 2½ lb. (about 3 medium)
Parchment paper
Unsalted butter, ¼ cup
White miso, 2 Tbsp.
Heavy cream, 2 Tbsp.
Kosher salt, ¼ tsp.
Freshly ground black pepper, ¼ tsp.

❶ Preheat oven to 450°. Scrub potatoes; pat dry, and place on a parchment paper-lined baking sheet. Bake at 450° for 1 hour or until tender. Let stand until cool enough to handle. Remove skins from potatoes.

❷ Press potatoes through a food mill into a bowl. Place potato, butter, and remaining ingredients in a medium saucepan; cook over medium-low heat, stirring often, 8 minutes or until hot. 4 servings

Note: If you don't have a food mill, process peeled cooked potato, butter, and remaining ingredients in a food processor until smooth. Transfer to a saucepan, and heat as directed in recipe.

miso (MEE-soh) n. Fermented soybean paste that also contains rice or barley and is used as a flavoring in Japanese dishes. Miso comes in different strengths and flavors; generally, the darker the color, the stronger the taste.

"It's nice to change things up now and then. So surprise people with this puree instead of the usual mashed potatoes. Cooking parsnips in milk imparts a subtle flavor and creamy texture. Plus, they hold really well so you can make them in advance. Reheat over low heat with a splash of milk before serving."

milk + butter + pepper

Parsnip Puree

1 Bring parsnips and 1½ cups milk to a simmer in a medium saucepan over medium-high heat, stirring occasionally. Reduce heat to medium low, and cook 10 minutes or until parsnips are tender. Place parsnips in a blender, using a slotted spoon. Add butter, salt, and pepper. Add remaining 1 cup milk through center cap with blender running; process until smooth. Return parsnip mixture to pan. Cook over medium heat 2 minutes or until thoroughly heated and consistency of mashed potatoes. 8 servings

Parsnips, 5 cups 2-inch pieces (about 6)
Milk, 2½ cups, divided
Unsalted butter, ¼ cup
Kosher salt, 1 tsp.
Freshly ground black pepper, ½ tsp.

Starches

Welcome to the feel-good chapter of this book! Starches and grains are a cherished part of the human diet. That's why I try to offer some sort of grain or starch with every meal.

For thousands of years, foods made from grain have been a constant. Think of comfort foods and what comes to mind? For me, it's the wheat used in North African couscous; the starchy, short-grain Arborio or Carnaroli rice that provides the foundation of Italian risotto; and certainly the varied pasta shapes made from durum wheat semolina. I couldn't imagine life without them.

"When rice became scarce in the mid-20th century, Israel's first prime minister, David Ben-Gurion, asked a food company to develop a wheat-based substitute. They created *ptitim,* now commonly known as Israeli couscous. Israeli couscous, with its bigger grains, is easier to work with than Moroccan, and I combine it with some of the most vibrant Mediterranean flavors around: green olives, pine nuts, and pre-served lemon."

Fine sea salt, 2½ tsp., divided

Israeli couscous, 3 cups uncooked

Pine nuts, 1 cup

Sicilian-style pitted olives, ¾ cup chopped

Preserved lemon, 1 thinly sliced (about ¼ cup)

Extra virgin olive oil, ¼ cup

Fresh lemon juice, 2 Tbsp.

Freshly ground black pepper, ½ tsp.

Israeli Couscous

1 Bring 6¾ cups water and 2 tsp. salt to a boil in a large saucepan; add couscous. Bring to a boil; cover, reduce heat, and cook 12 minutes or until couscous is tender and liquid is nearly absorbed. Drain.

2 Place nuts in a small nonstick skillet over medium-low heat; cook, stirring often, 5 to 7 minutes or until lightly browned and fragrant.

3 Place couscous in a large bowl. Add remaining ½ tsp. salt, pine nuts, olives, and remaining ingredients; toss well. 8 servings

Note: You may substitute the zest from 1 lemon for the preserved lemon slices, if desired.

Drink: Muscat

"Here, I blend Israeli couscous with sweet, chewy raisins, meaty mushrooms, and chickpeas—with a little crumbled Greek feta cheese thrown in for salt and texture. It makes a perfect vegetarian entrée served with crusty bread, a salad, and a bottle of earthy red wine."

onion

wild mushrooms

raisins

feta

Wild Mushroom Couscous

❶ Sauté onion and garlic in 2 Tbsp. olive oil in a 3-qt. saucepan over medium heat 3 minutes or until tender. Add mushrooms, and sauté 4 minutes. Stir in broth, couscous, salt, and pepper. Bring to a boil; cover, reduce heat, and cook, stirring occasionally, 15 minutes or just until pasta is tender and liquid is almost absorbed. Transfer couscous mixture to a large jelly-roll pan; cool 10 minutes. Place couscous in a large bowl; separate any lumps.

❷ Sauté chickpeas and raisins in remaining 1 Tbsp. oil in a medium skillet over medium heat 3 minutes or until thoroughly heated. Add chickpeas and raisins to couscous mixture; toss gently. Sprinkle with cheese. 8 servings

Drink: French Burgundy or Pinot Noir

Onion, ¼ cup finely chopped
Garlic, 2 cloves minced
Olive oil, 3 Tbsp., divided
Assorted fresh wild mushrooms, 3 cups
   sliced
Vegetable broth, 4 cups
Israeli couscous, 2 cups uncooked
Kosher salt, ¼ tsp.
Freshly ground black pepper, ⅛ tsp.
Chickpeas, canned ½ cup drained
Raisins, ½ cup
Feta cheese, ½ cup crumbled

"Clean and bright and so easy to make, this dish reflects the simple pleasures of Greek cooking in one bite. Serve it with my Greek Island Lamb Chops (page 175) for an easy al fresco dinner."

Orzo, 1 (12-oz.) package uncooked
Frozen petite peas, 3 cups cooked, divided
Feta cheese, 1 cup crumbled, divided
Fresh mint, ½ cup chopped, divided
Extra virgin olive oil, 3 Tbsp.
Freshly ground black pepper, ¼ tsp.
Kosher salt to taste
Garnish: fresh mint sprig

peas + feta + olive oil + mint

Orzo with Feta Cheese and Mint

❶ Cook orzo in boiling salted water according to package directions. Drain.

❷ Place orzo, 2½ cups peas, ¾ cup feta, ¼ cup mint, olive oil, and pepper in a medium bowl; toss gently. Sprinkle with remaining peas, feta, and mint. Taste and season with salt and more pepper to taste. Garnish, if desired. 6 servings

Drink: American Pale Ale or Washington Merlot, if served with the Greek Island Lamb Chops (page 175)

"Farro is the unhybridized ancestor of modern wheat that has been eaten in Europe and the Middle East since ancient times. It has a nutty flavor and creamy texture when cooked. I think it is a wonderful substitute for the usual bulgur in tabbouleh. It is definitely a worthy addition to your pantry. It is my grain of choice."

sherry   lemon juice   sumac   paprika
vinegar

Farro Tabbouleh

① Place farro in a colander. Rinse under cold running water; drain and place in a stockpot. Add water to 3 inches above farro. Add 2 Tbsp. salt, and bring to a boil; reduce heat, cover, and cook 25 minutes or just until tender. Drain and rinse under cold running water; drain and place in a large bowl.

② Combine oil, next 5 ingredients, and remaining 1 tsp. salt in a bowl; stir with a whisk. Add dressing to farro, tossing to coat. Add tomato and remaining ingredients; toss gently. 6 servings

Drink: French Sancerre

Farro, 1 lb.
Kosher salt, 2 Tbsp. plus 1 tsp., divided
Olive oil, 1 cup
Sherry vinegar, 2 Tbsp.
Fresh lemon juice, 2 Tbsp.
Ground sumac, ½ tsp.
Paprika, ½ tsp.
Freshly ground black pepper, ½ tsp.
Tomato, 1 cup seeded and diced
Cucumber, ¾ cup (½-inch) peeled, seeded, and cubed
Red onion, ¾ cup chopped
Fennel, ¾ cup chopped
Fresh flat-leaf parsley, ¼ cup chopped
Jalapeño pepper, 2 Tbsp. seeded and minced

"I've been known for my polenta for years, but using semolina is a fresh take on a classic. This takes only a few minutes to make and is the perfect base for my Slow-Roasted Pork (page 183), Tequila-Braised Short Ribs (page 172), or Chicken Under a Brick (page 144)."

Parmigiano-Reggiano + kosher salt + cream

Semolina Polenta

Milk, 3 cups

Semolina or pasta flour, 1 cup

Parmigiano-Reggiano cheese, ½ cup freshly grated

Kosher salt and freshly ground pepper to taste

Heavy cream, ⅓ cup (optional)

❶ Cook milk in a heavy nonaluminum saucepan over medium heat, stirring often, 6 minutes or just until bubbles appear (do not boil). Stir in semolina. Cook, stirring constantly, 2 minutes or just until semolina begins to set. Stir in ½ cup cheese and salt and pepper to taste. If desired, whisk in up to ⅓ cup cream for desired consistency. 4 servings

Note: I suggest using Bob's Red Mill Semolina Flour.

Drink: Friulian Italian white

"Meat and potatoes is a classic combination; adding protein to your mashed potatoes—not so much. Chorizo is a flavorful addition. Orange juice provides a bright foil for the sausage's richness. Smoked paprika gives this a distinctly Spanish flavor."

cream + smoked chorizo + smoked paprika + orange juice

Chorizo Mashed Potatoes

❶ Cook potatoes and ½ tsp. salt in boiling water to cover 15 minutes or until tender.

❷ While potatoes cook, combine 2 Tbsp. cream and butter in a small saucepan. Cook over medium heat 2 minutes or until warm. Add butter mixture to potatoes; mash with a potato masher until chunky. Cover and keep warm.

❸ Cook sausage, shallot, and paprika in oil in a medium saucepan over medium heat, stirring constantly, 10 minutes or until sausage softens. Increase heat to medium-high; add orange juice, stirring to loosen particles from bottom of pan. Add remaining cream; cook, stirring often, 15 minutes or until liquid is reduced by half. Remove from heat; cool 5 minutes.

❹ Place sausage mixture in a blender; process until consistency of thick soup. Add sausage mixture, remaining 1 tsp. salt, and pepper to mashed potatoes; mash with a potato masher until desired consistency. 4 servings

Baking potatoes, 2 lb. cut into 1½-inch cubes
Kosher salt, 1½ tsp., divided
Heavy cream, 2 cups, divided
Unsalted butter, 2 Tbsp.
Smoked chorizo, 8 oz. casings removed and cut into 1½-inch slices
Shallot, 1 finely chopped
Smoked paprika, 1 Tbsp.
Canola oil, 2 Tbsp.
Fresh orange juice, ½ cup
Freshly ground black pepper, ¼ tsp.

drink: Italian Corvina (Ripasso)

"I always use this risotto recipe, adding seasonal ingredients that inspire me. In the fall, it might be butternut squash or wild mushrooms; in the spring, peas or asparagus. I prefer risotto Venetian-style, a bit soupier and more al dente than normal.

For creamy risotto that isn't starchy, you must maintain the broth at simmer so that as you make additions, you do not stop the cooking process by adding a cold liquid. I give an approximate amount of chicken broth here—the amount will always vary. Taste the rice toward the end of cooking, and add broth in smaller amounts until the grains are just al dente."

onion + white wine + butter + Parmigiano-Reggiano

Master Risotto

1 Heat chicken broth in a medium saucepan over low heat until warm. Keep warm.

2 Cook onion in oil in a medium saucepan over medium-low heat, stirring constantly, 9 minutes or until tender. Add rice, stirring to coat. Cook rice, stirring often, 4 minutes (do not brown). Increase heat to medium; stir in wine. Cook, stirring constantly, 2 minutes or until wine is absorbed.

3 Add 1 cup warm broth, stirring constantly, until liquid is absorbed. Repeat procedure with remaining broth, adding 1 cup at a time, until liquid is absorbed. (Total cooking time is about 22 minutes.)

4 Add butter, stirring until melted. Remove from heat; stir in cheese. Let stand, uncovered, 5 minutes before serving. Serve immediately. 6 servings

Chicken broth, 7 cups
Onion, 1 small diced (about 1 cup)
Olive oil, ¼ cup
Arborio rice, 3 cups uncooked
Dry white wine, 1 cup
Unsalted butter, ½ cup
Parmigiano-Reggiano cheese, ⅔ cup
   freshly grated

Drink: Northern Italian white wine

Halve: With a very sharp knife, carefully slice the onion in half through the root and stem end.

Peel: Once halved, peel away the onion's papery skin and discard before cutting the onion as required for your recipe.

Cut: Working cut side down, make a series of horizontal cuts almost to the root end. Then make parallel cuts down through the layers from top to bottom.

Dice: Holding the sliced onion securely from the root end just behind the knife blade, cut across the grain to make a perfectly uniform dice.

ginger + carrot juice + Parmigiano-Reggiano + rosemary

"I love freshly-extracted juices, but you can purchase carrot juice at the grocery store. If you juice your own, toss in a coin-size piece of ginger for an added zing."

Carrots, 1 lb. small with greenery

Olive oil, 5 Tbsp., divided

Chicken broth, 3⅔ cups, divided

Unsalted butter, ½ cup cold cut up, divided

Honey, 2 Tbsp.

Fresh ginger, 2 tsp. minced

Carrot juice, 2⅔ cups

Onion, 1 cup finely chopped

Arborio rice, 2¼ cups

Dry white wine, 1 cup

Parmigiano-Reggiano cheese, ½ cup freshly grated

Fresh ginger, 1 Tbsp. grated

Kosher salt, ¼ tsp.

Fresh rosemary, 2 Tbsp. chopped

Garnish: shaved Parmigiano-Reggiano cheese

Double-Carrot Risotto

1 Scrub carrots under cold running water; pat dry. Cook carrots in 2 Tbsp. olive oil in a large skillet over medium heat 12 minutes or until lightly browned. Turn carrots over; cook 6 minutes or until lightly browned. Add ¼ cup broth; cover and cook 7 minutes or until carrots are tender. Remove carrots from pan. Add 2 Tbsp. butter, honey, and 2 tsp. minced ginger to pan; cook, stirring constantly, 2 minutes. Return carrots to pan, stirring to coat. Remove pan from heat.

2 Heat remaining chicken broth and carrot juice in a medium saucepan over medium heat until warm. Keep warm.

3 Sauté onion in remaining 3 Tbsp. olive oil in a large saucepan over medium heat 7 minutes or until tender. Add rice, stirring to coat. Cook rice, stirring often, 3 minutes (do not brown). Stir in wine. Cook, stirring constantly, 1 minute or until wine is absorbed.

4 Add 2 cups warm broth mixture, stirring constantly, until liquid is absorbed. Repeat procedure with remaining broth mixture, adding 1 cup at a time, until liquid is absorbed. (Total cooking time is about 30 minutes.) Remove pan from heat. Add remaining 6 Tbsp. butter, ½ cup grated cheese, 1 Tbsp. grated ginger, and salt, stirring until butter and cheese melt. Cover and let stand 3 minutes.

5 Cut carrots in half lengthwise. Spoon risotto onto serving plates. Sprinkle with rosemary, and top with halved carrots. Garnish, if desired. Serve immediately.
6 servings

Drink: Artisanal Ginger Beer (nonalcoholic)

rosemary + orange zest + Parmigiano-Reggiano + blue cheese

Beet Risotto with Blue Cheese

1 Preheat oven to 425°. Cut tops off beets, leaving 1 inch greenery on each. Scrub beets under cold running water; pat dry. Cut each beet, lengthwise, into 3 wedges, leaving a portion of greenery on each wedge. Place beets in a large bowl; drizzle with 2 Tbsp. olive oil, and sprinkle with 1 Tbsp. rosemary, 1 tsp. orange zest, 1 tsp. salt, and pepper. Toss to coat. Line a large jelly-roll pan with aluminum foil; lightly grease foil. Place beets in a single layer on prepared pan. Bake at 425° for 35 minutes or until beets are tender, turning once.

2 Heat chicken broth and beet juice in a medium saucepan over medium heat until warm; keep warm.

3 Sauté onion in remaining 3 Tbsp. olive oil in a large saucepan over medium heat 7 minutes or until tender. Add rice, stirring to coat. Cook rice, stirring often, 3 minutes (do not brown). Stir in wine. Cook, stirring constantly, 1 minute or until wine is absorbed.

4 Add 2 cups warm broth mixture, stirring constantly, until liquid is absorbed. Repeat procedure with remaining broth mixture, 1 cup at a time, until liquid is absorbed. (Total cooking time is about 28 minutes.) Remove pan from heat.

5 Add remaining 1 Tbsp. rosemary, remaining 1 tsp. orange zest, remaining ½ tsp. salt, Parmigiano-Reggiano cheese, and butter, stirring until cheese and butter melt. Cover and let stand 3 minutes.

6 Pour risotto onto serving plates. Place 3 beet wedges on each serving, and sprinkle evenly with blue cheese. Garnish, if desired. Serve immediately. 6 servings

Drink: California Petit Verdot

"The Venetians have a word for the ideal consistency of risotto: *alla onda,* which means 'like a wave.' You should be able to pour the risotto onto the plate, where it will set slightly."

Fresh beets, 6 medium with greenery (about 1¾ lb.)
Extra virgin olive oil, 5 Tbsp., divided
Fresh rosemary, 2 Tbsp. chopped, divided
Orange zest, 2 tsp., divided
Kosher salt, 1½ tsp., divided
Freshly ground black pepper, ½ tsp.
Chicken broth, 3⅔ cups
Beet juice, 2⅓ cups
Onion, 1 cup finely chopped
Arborio rice, 2¼ cups
Dry white wine, 1 cup
Parmigiano-Reggiano cheese, ½ cup freshly grated
Unsalted butter, 6 Tbsp.
Blue cheese, 1 cup crumbled
Garnish: fresh rosemary sprig

"The sweet, briny flavor of shrimp marries seamlessly with the salty, fruity flavor of olives in this quick and easy pasta dish. There are so many wonderful tapenades on store shelves today that you don't have to bother making your own."

garlic   +   tomatoes   +   fresh basil   +   olive tapenade

Pasta with Shrimp and Olive Sauce

Fettuccine, 12 oz. uncooked
Garlic, 10 cloves thinly sliced
Extra virgin olive oil, ½ cup
Dried crushed red pepper, 1 tsp.
Large shrimp, 2 lb. raw peeled and deveined
Tomatoes, 1 lb. cut into ½-inch pieces (about 3 cups)
Fresh basil leaves, ⅔ cup loosely packed and torn
Fresh lemon juice, 3 Tbsp.
Freshly ground black pepper, 1 tsp.
Kosher salt, ½ tsp.
Olive tapenade, 1 (7-oz.) container
Garnish: fresh basil leaves

1 Cook pasta in boiling salted water according to package directions. Drain and place in a large bowl.

2 While pasta cooks, cook garlic in olive oil in a large skillet over medium-low heat, stirring occasionally, 10 minutes. Stir in crushed red pepper; cook, stirring occasionally, 5 minutes. Increase heat to medium-high. Add shrimp; cook 3 to 5 minutes or until shrimp turn pink. Pour shrimp mixture over pasta. Add tomato and next 5 ingredients; toss gently. Garnish, if desired. 8 servings

Drink: Oregon Pinot Noir

"Classic Cacio e Pepe (cheese and pepper) is one of my favorite pasta dishes. It's the perfect balance of creamy, tart, spicy, and overall delicious. Adding baby artichokes is just 'gravy.' Make this once, and it will become a standby."

 +  + +

walnuts   *Pecorino Romano*   *pepper*   *lemon zest*

Carciofi Cacio e Pepe (Artichoke Cheese-and-Pepper Pasta)

1 Preheat oven to 350°. Cut off stem ends, and trim about ½ inch from top of each artichoke. Remove any loose bottom leaves. Trim one fourth off top of each outer leaf with scissors. Quarter artichokes lengthwise.

2 Place walnuts in a single layer in a shallow pan. Bake at 350° for 12 to 14 minutes or until lightly toasted and fragrant, stirring halfway through. Cool completely; roughly chop. Increase oven temperature to 425°.

3 Arrange artichokes in a steamer basket over boiling water. Cover and steam 10 to 12 minutes or until tender. Drain well. Toss artichokes with 2 Tbsp. olive oil, ½ tsp. salt, and ¼ tsp. pepper. Arrange on baking sheet, and roast at 425° for 10 minutes or until golden brown, stirring halfway through. Remove from oven.

4 Meanwhile, cook pasta in boiling salted water according to package directions; drain. In a large bowl, combine pasta, artichokes, walnuts, 2 cups cheese, parsley, lemon zest, remaining 2 Tbsp. olive oil, and remaining salt and pepper. Toss gently to combine. Serve in shallow bowls with extra Pecorino Romano, if desired. 6 servings

drink: Oregon Pinot Blanc

Baby artichokes, 1 lb.
Walnut halves, ⅔ cup
Olive oil, ¼ cup, divided
Kosher salt, 1½ tsp., divided
Freshly ground black pepper, 1¼ tsp., divided
Spaghetti, 12 oz. uncooked
Pecorino Romano cheese, 2 cups freshly grated
Fresh parsley, ½ cup chopped
Fresh lemon zest, 1½ tsp.

"Mushrooms prepared in the simplest of ways with shallots, wine, and rosemary tossed in a tangle of homemade pasta—this dish truly is dreamy. The sauce is perfect for pairing with my Fresh Semolina Pasta (page 35)."

assorted mushrooms + *shallots* + *white wine* + *rosemary*

Olive oil, 3 Tbsp.

Assorted mushrooms, 12 oz. cut into ½-inch-thick slices

Kosher salt to taste

Freshly ground black pepper to taste

Shallots, ¼ cup finely diced

Dry white wine, ½ cup

Fresh rosemary, 1 to 2 Tbsp. chopped

Fresh Semolina Pasta (page 35), cut into pappardelle or fettuccine

Unsalted butter, 6 Tbsp.

Parmigiano-Reggiano cheese, ⅓ cup freshly grated

Drink: Hefeweizen

Pappardelle Pasta with Dreamy Mushroom Sauce

❶ Heat olive oil in a large pan over medium-low heat. Add mushrooms, sprinkle with desired amount of salt and pepper, and sauté, without stirring, 5 minutes. (Reduce heat to low, if necessary, to avoid burning. Mushrooms will release their liquid while cooking, and then begin to reabsorb it.) Stir in shallots and white wine, and increase heat to medium. Sauté 3 minutes or until shallots are soft and most of wine is absorbed. Stir in rosemary.

❷ Meanwhile, cook pasta, reserving some cooking liquid. Add cooked pasta to mushroom mixture in pan. Add butter, stirring until melted. Stir in a small amount of reserved cooking liquid, if desired. Stir in salt and pepper to taste, and place in a large serving bowl or individual serving bowls. Sprinkle with cheese, and serve immediately. 4 servings

Combine flours and salt on a work surface; make a well in center. Place eggs and egg yolks in center of flour well. Whisk eggs with a fork, gradually stirring in flour from bottom and sides of well into the center until mixture becomes very stiff. Knead dough on a lightly floured surface 10 minutes or until smooth. Wrap in plastic and chill 30 minutes before rolling out and cutting as desired.

corn + ricotta + butter

"Ravioli is all about the filling, so the dough should be really thin. Buy prepared dough if you'd rather."

Sweet Corn Ravioli

1 Combine first 3 ingredients in a large bowl, stirring until well blended.

2 Divide pasta dough into 6 equal portions, keeping reserved dough covered to prevent drying. Working with 1 portion at a time, shape each portion into a disk. Slightly flatten disk, and pass through smooth rollers of pasta machine on widest setting. Fold short ends in toward the center, forming a rectangle; pass through next smaller setting. Pass dough once through rollers 2 through 6. Repeat procedure until dough has reached a 6 x 18–inch rectangle.

3 Lay rectangle horizontally on a lightly floured work surface. Beginning at top left corner of dough (1 inch down and 1 inch over), spoon about 1 Tbsp. corn mixture in a small mound on dough. Make a second mound in a straight line 2 inches to the right of first mound. Repeat for a total of 6 equal mounds across top half of rectangle. Brush bottom half of dough with water. Fold bottom half of rectangle up over top half, pressing between mounds to seal into 6 squares. Cut between mounds to form 6 filled squares of dough. Repeat procedure with remaining dough and filling.

4 Bring 4 qt. water and 2 tsp. salt to a boil in a 6-qt. Dutch oven. Add ravioli, and cook 3 to 4 minutes or until pasta is al dente; drain.

5 Melt butter in a large saucepan over medium-low heat. Cook just until butter begins to brown and has a nutty fragrance. Add 6 ravioli to butter, turning to coat; remove to a serving dish. Repeat procedure with remaining ravioli. Serve immediately. 6 servings

Creamed Corn (page 101), 2½ cups
Ricotta cheese, ½ cup
Panko breadcrumbs, 3 Tbsp.
Fresh Semolina Pasta dough (page 35),
   uncooked
Kosher salt, 2 tsp.
Unsalted butter, ½ cup

Drink: New Zealand chardonnay

Dust your work surface very lightly with flour and arrange the rectangle of prepared pasta dough horizontally in front of you.

Mound tablespoonfuls of the corn mixture about 1 inch from the top of the dough and at 1-inch intervals, for a total of 6 mounds of filling.

Fold the bottom half of the dough up and over the filling after lightly brushing the dough with water to help it stick together.

Press between the mounds gently on all sides to seal the "pockets" of filling into 6 equal squares.

Cut evenly between the mounds of filling with a sharp knife or pastry cutter so that each mound has an equal frame of dough.

Repeat procedure with remaining dough and filling until all the ravioli have been formed and are ready to cook.

"I grew up in Georgia, and this spoon bread takes me right back to my childhood, when eating fried oysters and spoon bread on the coast near Savannah was a regular meal. This is an incredible side dish for Fried Chicken My Way (page 145) or my Bluefish Saltimbocca (page 197)."

corn + eggs + butter + honey

Corn Spoon Bread

Milk, 4 cups

Stone-ground yellow cornmeal, 2 cups

Fresh corn kernels, 2 cups

Sugar, ¼ cup

Baking powder, 1 Tbsp.

Kosher salt, 2 tsp.

Large egg whites, 3

Large eggs, 3

Unsalted butter, ½ cup, divided

Honey, 1 Tbsp.

❶ Preheat oven to 375°. Combine milk and cornmeal in a medium saucepan, stirring with a whisk. Cook over medium-high heat, stirring often, 10 minutes or until mixture thickens. Remove from heat, and stir in corn kernels.

❷ Combine sugar, baking powder, and salt in a medium bowl. Add cornmeal mixture, stirring with a whisk.

❸ Beat egg whites at high speed with an electric mixer until stiff peaks form. Add eggs to cornmeal batter, stirring with a whisk; fold in egg whites.

❹ Heat a 12-inch cast-iron skillet over medium-high heat until hot. Add ¼ cup butter to pan, tilting to coat bottom. Cook over medium-low heat 3 minutes or until butter begins to brown. Pour batter into pan. Bake at 375° for 25 to 30 minutes or until set.

❺ While spoon bread bakes, combine remaining ¼ cup butter and honey in a small saucepan. Cook, stirring constantly, over medium heat 2 minutes or until butter melts. Drizzle honey butter over top of bread. Serve immediately. 10 to 12 servings

Drink: English Stout

Birds and Eggs

Which came first, the chicken or the egg? It really doesn't matter because I love poultry in all forms. When shopping for poultry, I like to spend a little extra money and look for birds that are free-range and given no hormones. You'll notice a difference in the flavor of the meat. And isn't it amazing to see the resurgence of people raising chickens at home? I love the assortment of eggs available these days, and welcome only the freshest ones I can get my hands on for cooking. Choose organic eggs from free-range birds fed a natural diet. The raw yolk should be a rich golden yellow and sit plumply above the egg white when cracked into a bowl. Enjoy them innumerable ways—scrambled, poached, or in frittatas and omelets. Eggs are a perfect food.

"I'm a huge lover of chili. Chicken lightens up this version but maintains the classic flavors you expect from a hearty bowl of stew. I love to use beer as a braising liquid, and there's nothing better on a cold day than a warm bowl of chili and a cold pint of beer. (I like this on a hot day, too, just not with hot beer!)"

ancho chile powder + *beer* + *cilantro* + *rosemary*

Chicken Chili

Ground chicken, 1 lb.
Yellow onion, 1½ cups chopped
Garlic, 2 Tbsp. minced (about 4 cloves)
Canola oil, 1 Tbsp.
Ancho chile powder, 2 Tbsp.
Ground cumin, 1½ tsp.
Kosher salt, 1 tsp.
Chicken broth, 2 cups
Beer, 1 (12-oz.) bottle
Chopped tomatoes, 1 (14.5-oz.) can
    undrained
White beans, 1 (15.5-oz.) can drained and
    rinsed
Fresh cilantro, 2 Tbsp. chopped
Fresh rosemary, 2 Tbsp. chopped
Kosher salt and freshly ground black
    pepper to taste
Garnish: shredded mild Cheddar cheese,
    lime wedges

❶ Cook first 3 ingredients in hot oil in a large Dutch oven over medium-high heat, stirring often, 12 to 13 minutes or until meat crumbles and is no longer pink. Stir in chile powder and next 2 ingredients, and cook 1 minute. Add broth and next 2 ingredients, and bring to a boil. Reduce heat to low, and simmer, uncovered, stirring occasionally, 30 minutes. Stir in beans, and cook 5 minutes or until thoroughly heated.

❷ Remove from heat, and stir in cilantro and rosemary. Season with salt and pepper to taste. Garnish, if desired. 4 servings

Drink: American Red Ale

"When I started cooking, Chicken Cordon Bleu was all the rage, and it's one of those dishes that has stood up well to the test of time. This is a lighter, quicker version to make at home."

Dijon mustard + Swiss cheese + pancetta

Chicken Cordon Bleu

❶ Preheat broiler with oven rack 4 inches from heat. Butterfly chicken breasts by making a lengthwise cut in 1 side of each, cutting through the opposite side; unfold. Sprinkle with salt and pepper.

❷ Cook chicken in hot oil in a large sauté pan 5 minutes on each side or until well browned and done.

❸ Transfer chicken to a baking sheet, and spread tops with mustard. Top with Swiss cheese and pancetta. Broil 3 minutes or until cheese is melted and pancetta is crisp. Serve immediately. 4 servings

Drink: California Pinot Noir

Skinned and boned chicken breasts, 2 (about 1½ lb.)

Kosher salt, 1 tsp.

Freshly ground black pepper, 1 tsp.

Olive oil, 2 Tbsp.

Dijon mustard, 1 Tbsp.

Swiss cheese, 4 (0.7-oz.) slices

Pancetta, 8 very thin slices (about 2 oz.)

"There is a restaurant on the outskirts of Bangkok called Soi Polo. When I was there taping my TV show, I went to this restaurant three times for this dish. Fried garlic, fried shallots, and spice-infused chicken made it impossible to stay away! Seems others agree with me. The restaurant has become world famous for this chicken. Here's my version for you."

soy sauce + *ginger* + *shallots* + *jalapeño pepper*

Soi Polo Chicken Thighs

Soy sauce or tamari, 1 cup
Sweet rice wine, 3 Tbsp.
Brown sugar, 3 Tbsp.
Dark sesame oil, 2 Tbsp.
Fresh ginger, 1 Tbsp. chopped
Skin-on, boned chicken thighs,
  8 (about 3 lb.)
Vegetable or canola oil
Shallots, 1½ cups thinly sliced (about 5 large)
All-purpose flour, 1 cup
Garlic, 3 Tbsp. thinly sliced (about 5 cloves)
Jalapeño pepper, 1 thinly sliced
Kosher salt and freshly ground black
  pepper to taste
Fresh cilantro, 3 Tbsp. chopped

1 Whisk together first 5 ingredients in a shallow dish or zip-top plastic freezer bag; add chicken, turning to coat. Cover or seal, and chill 30 minutes to 3 hours.

2 Preheat oven to 375°. Lightly grease a 13- x 9-inch baking dish. Remove chicken from marinade, discarding marinade. Place chicken, skin sides up, in prepared baking dish. Bake at 375° for 40 minutes or until done and skin is golden brown.

3 Meanwhile, pour oil to a depth of 2 inches into a Dutch oven; heat over medium-high heat to 350°. Lightly dredge shallots in flour, shaking off excess. Fry shallots, in batches, 1 to 2 minutes or just until crispy. Drain on a paper towel-lined baking sheet. Repeat procedure with garlic and jalapeño pepper. Sprinkle shallots, garlic, and jalapeño pepper generously with salt and pepper to taste.

4 Divide chicken among individual serving plates. Sprinkle with shallots, garlic, jalapeño pepper, and cilantro. Serve immediately. 4 servings

Drink: Junmai Sake

"I've always loved traditional beef stroganoff, but swap the beef for chicken, and it is dyn-o-mite! It comes together so quickly on a weeknight."

shiitake mushrooms + cognac + thyme + cream

Chicken Stroganoff

1 Sprinkle chicken with 1 tsp. salt and ½ tsp. pepper. Cook in hot oil in a large sauté pan over medium-high heat, stirring often, 7 minutes or until done. Remove from pan.

2 Melt butter in pan. Add mushrooms and shallots, and sauté 5 minutes or until mushrooms release their liquid and begin to soften. Stir in thyme and dry mustard. Cook 1 minute.

3 Remove pan from heat; stir in cognac, and carefully ignite the fumes just above mixture with a long match or long multipurpose lighter. Let flames die down.

4 Prepare pasta according to package directions.

5 Meanwhile, return pan to heat; cook over medium heat, stirring often, until liquid is reduced to about 1 Tbsp. Stir in broth, and cook 5 to 7 minutes or until reduced by half. Reduce heat to low, and stir in cream and Dijon mustard. Cook, stirring often, 10 minutes or until reduced by half. Return chicken to pan. Cook 1 to 2 minutes or until thoroughly heated. Sprinkle with remaining ½ tsp. salt and ½ tsp. pepper. Pour chicken-and-sauce mixture over hot cooked pasta, and toss to coat. Serve immediately. 4 servings

Drink: Oregon Chardonnay

Skinned and boned
   chicken breasts, 1 lb. cut into
   1-inch cubes
Kosher salt, 1½ tsp., divided
Freshly ground black pepper, 1 tsp., divided
Olive oil, 2 Tbsp.
Unsalted butter, 2 Tbsp.
Shiitake mushrooms, 1 lb. stemmed and
   sliced
Shallots, 2 minced
Fresh thyme leaves, 2 Tbsp.
Dry mustard, 1 tsp.
Cognac, ½ cup
Wide egg noodles, 1 (16-oz.) package
Chicken broth, 1½ cups
Heavy cream, 1 cup
Dijon mustard, 1 Tbsp.

"The trick for an amazing, perfectly cooked chicken breast is to pound it so it cooks quickly, and to start it skin side down in the pan with a brick on top. Don't touch it for five minutes; this creates flavorful crisped skin. Then all you have to do is flip it over for one minute to 'kiss it,' or let it finish cooking. There's no need to buy any fancy equipment for this. All it takes is a foil-covered brick or two, and voilà!"

Berbere Spice Blend + *pepper* + *olive oil*

Chicken Under a Brick

Skin-on, boned chicken breasts, 2 (about 6 oz. each)
Berbere Spice Blend (page 21), ½ tsp.
Kosher salt and freshly ground black pepper to taste
Olive oil, 1 Tbsp.
Bricks, 2 wrapped in aluminum foil

Drink: California white blend

❶ Place chicken, skin sides down, between 2 sheets of plastic wrap, and flatten to ½-inch thickness, using a rolling pin or flat side of a meat mallet. Sprinkle chicken with Berbere Spice Blend and desired amount of salt and pepper.

❷ Heat oil in a large skillet over medium-high heat. Add chicken, skin sides down, and top each with an aluminum foil-wrapped brick. Cook 5 minutes or until skin is very crispy and chicken is almost done. Remove bricks, flip chicken, and cook 1 minute or until chicken is done. Transfer to a serving dish, and let stand 5 minutes. 2 servings

Chicken Under a Brick Salad: Prepare recipe as directed. Toss 6 cups (10 oz.) mixed baby greens with my Basic Vinaigrette (page 16). Slice chicken, and place over salad. 4 servings

yogurt + paprika + bacon

Fried Chicken My Way

1 Whisk together yogurt and milk in a large shallow dish.

2 Add chicken to yogurt mixture; cover and chill 2 to 4 hours.

3 Stir together flour, paprika, pepper, and 1 tsp. salt in a large shallow dish.

4 Remove chicken from yogurt mixture, discarding yogurt mixture. Rinse chicken, and pat dry. Dredge chicken in flour mixture, shaking off excess.

5 Pour oil to a depth of 1½ inches into a 12-inch cast-iron skillet; heat over medium-high heat to 350°. Fry bacon in hot oil 2 to 3 minutes or until crisp. Transfer to paper towels; crumble bacon.

6 Fry chicken, in batches, in hot oil 8 to 9 minutes on each side or until done (a meat thermometer inserted into thickest portion of breast should register 170°). Drain on a wire rack over paper towels. Sprinkle with remaining 1 tsp. salt.

7 Serve chicken sprinkled with crumbled bacon. 4 servings

"Growing up in the South, I remember there was always an occasion for fried chicken. It's 90% about the crunch and 10% about the seasonings. Here, oil and rendered bacon fat are a more everyday stand-in for the traditional lard. Use Rosemary-Maple Butter Sauce (page 149) as a dip."

Plain yogurt, 2 cups
Milk, 1 cup
Whole chicken, 1 (2½-lb.) cut-up
All-purpose flour, 2 cups
Hungarian paprika, 1 Tbsp.
Freshly ground black pepper, 1 tsp.
Kosher salt, 2 tsp., divided
Vegetable oil
Thick-cut bacon, 4 slices

Drink: IPA (India Pale Ale)

"I'm a food history nut who loves uncovering the origins of recipes. Originally, chicken cacciatore did not incorporate the tomatoes we assume. Instead, wine or vinegar was the base for the braise, so the sauce was quite dark. This version is inspired by a 15th-century recipe, and it is believed to be the predecessor of Coq au Vin."

shiitake mushrooms + shallots + red wine + balsamic vinegar

"Old School" Chicken Cacciatore

1 Sprinkle chicken with salt and pepper. Dredge in flour, shaking off excess.

2 Cook chicken, in batches, in 2 Tbsp. hot oil in a large Dutch oven over medium-high heat 3 to 5 minutes on each side or until browned. Transfer to a plate, and wipe Dutch oven clean.

3 Add remaining 2 Tbsp. oil to Dutch oven, and heat over medium heat. Add mushrooms and next 4 ingredients, and cook, stirring occasionally, 5 minutes or until mushrooms are soft. Return chicken to Dutch oven, and add wine and next 3 ingredients.

4 Bring to a simmer. Cover, reduce heat to low, and cook 1½ hours or until meat is tender enough to fall off the bone, basting chicken occasionally with liquid in Dutch oven. Remove and discard bay leaf. Season with salt and pepper to taste. Serve over Semolina Polenta; sprinkle with parsley just before serving. 4 to 6 servings

drink: Italian Barbera

Skinned, bone-in chicken thighs, 8 (about 4 lb.)
Kosher salt, 1 tsp.
Freshly ground black pepper, 1 tsp.
All-purpose flour, 1 cup
Olive oil, ¼ cup, divided
Shiitake mushrooms, 3 cups sliced
Shallots, ½ cup finely chopped
Anchovies, 2 coarsely chopped
Garlic, 3 cloves minced
Capers, 3 Tbsp. drained
Dry red wine, 2 cups
Balsamic vinegar, ⅓ cup
Fresh sage leaves, 4
Bay leaf, 1
Kosher salt and freshly ground black pepper to taste
Semolina Polenta (page 122)
Fresh flat-leaf parsley, ½ cup coarsely chopped

"A tomato base is what most of us think of when it comes to cacciatore. I prefer whole cut-up chicken for this dish, as it is incredibly inexpensive and gives everyone at the table a favored piece. Make this for company—do the braise ahead, and reheat it the next day; it will taste even better."

 + +  +

tomatoes   shiitake mushrooms   white wine   rosemary

"New School" Chicken Cacciatore

1 Drain tomatoes, reserving ½ cup juice.

2 If applicable, remove giblets from chicken, and reserve for another use. Rinse chicken, and pat dry. Sprinkle with 1 tsp. salt and 1 tsp. pepper.

3 Cook chicken, in batches, in hot oil in a large Dutch oven over medium-high heat 3 to 5 minutes on each side or until browned. Remove from Dutch oven.

4 Reduce heat to medium. Add shiitake mushrooms and next 3 ingredients to Dutch oven, and cook, stirring occasionally, 8 minutes or until mushrooms are soft and onion is translucent. Add wine, and bring to a boil. Cook 2 minutes. Add broth, rosemary, tomatoes, and reserved tomato juice, and bring to a boil. Return chicken to Dutch oven, nestling into sauce.

5 Cover and cook over medium-low heat 1½ hours or until meat is tender enough to fall off the bone, basting chicken occasionally with liquid in Dutch oven during cooking. Season with salt and pepper to taste. Sprinkle with parsley just before serving. 4 to 6 servings

Note: I highly recommend using San Marzano tomatoes in this dish. Other canned tomatoes are packed in a thinner juice.

Whole tomatoes, 1 (28-oz.) can undrained
Whole chicken, 1 (about 4 lb.) cut into 8 pieces
Kosher salt, 1 tsp.
Freshly ground black pepper, 1 tsp.
Olive oil, 2 Tbsp.
Shiitake mushrooms, 1½ cups sliced
Cremini mushrooms, 1½ cups sliced
Yellow onion, 1 large diced (about 2 cups)
Garlic, 3 cloves minced
Dry white wine, ½ cup
Chicken broth, 1½ cups
Fresh rosemary sprigs, 2 (4-inch)
Kosher salt and freshly ground black pepper to taste
Fresh flat-leaf parsley, ½ cup chopped

Drink: Italian Dolcetto d'Alba

"So often with turkey, the breast dries out before the dark meat finishes cooking. Butterflying the bird allows it to cook more evenly. Ask your butcher to do the work and flatten it for you. Always buy organic turkey—in order to avoid those injected with salt solutions—so that you can safely brine the bird at home. The technique adds flavor and moisture and works great with thick pork chops, too."

Kosher salt, 2½ cups
Maple syrup, 2½ cups
Whole peppercorns, ½ cup
Cold water, 16 cups
Bay leaves, 8
Fresh rosemary sprigs, 6
Fresh thyme sprigs, 10
Organic turkey, 1 (14-lb.) butterflied
Rosemary-Maple Butter Sauce
Garnish: fresh rosemary sprigs

Drink: Kentucky Maple (page 45)

maple syrup   +   bay leaves   +   rosemary   +   thyme

Grilled Maple-Brined Turkey with Rosemary-Maple Butter Sauce

1 To prepare brine, cook first 3 ingredients and 8 cups cold water in a 16-qt. stockpot over high heat, stirring occasionally, 2 minutes or until salt is dissolved. Remove from heat, and stir in bay leaves, next 2 ingredients, and remaining 8 cups cold water. Cool to room temperature. Add turkey; cover and chill 12 hours, weighing turkey down, if needed, to keep submerged.

2 Lightly grease 1 side of grill, and heat grill to 400° to 500° (high) heat; leave other side unlit. Remove turkey from brine, discarding brine. Pat turkey dry, and place, breast side down, over unlit side of grill. Grill over indirect heat, covered, 2 to 2½ hours or until skin is well browned and a meat thermometer inserted into thickest portion of thigh registers 165°. Flip turkey halfway through cook time. Shield with aluminum foil during last 30 minutes of grilling. Remove from grill, and let stand 20 minutes before carving. Serve turkey with Rosemary-Maple Butter Sauce. Garnish, if desired. 8 to 10 servings

Cut along both sides of the backbone; remove and discard giblets. Turn the bird breast-side up and press, breaking bones as necessary, to flatten. **Tuck** the wing tips under or break off and discard. Proceed as directed in Step 1 above.

rosemary-maple butter sauce:

Maple syrup, ½ cup
Unsalted butter, ½ cup

Fresh rosemary leaves, 2 Tbsp.
  coarsely chopped
Kosher salt to taste

1 Cook syrup, butter, and rosemary in a small saucepan over low heat, whisking often, 2 minutes or until butter is melted. Season with salt to taste. Serve turkey with sauce.

"Obviously, I like chili, because there's more than one version in this book! This rendition is as tasty as a taco…only served in a bowl with a spoon."

Mexican Spice Blend + onion + tomatoes + Monterey Jack

Turkey Chili

Ground turkey, 1 lb.
Vegetable oil, 1 Tbsp.
Onion, 1½ cups chopped
Mexican Spice Blend (page 20), 3 Tbsp.
Garlic, 6 cloves minced
Kosher salt, ½ tsp.
Diced green chiles, 1 (4.5-oz.) can
Diced tomatoes, 1 (29-oz.) can undrained
Light beer, 1 (12-oz.) can
Pinto beans, 2 (16-oz.) cans drained
Monterey Jack cheese, 1 cup (4 oz.)
   shredded
Fresh cilantro, ¼ cup chopped

Drink: Hefeweizen

❶ Cook turkey in hot oil in a Dutch oven over medium-high heat, stirring often, 10 to 12 minutes or until turkey crumbles and is no longer pink; drain. Add onion; sauté 3 minutes or until onion is tender. Stir in Mexican Spice Blend and next 3 ingredients; cook 1 minute. Stir in tomatoes and beer. Bring to a boil; reduce heat, and simmer, uncovered, 30 minutes.

❷ Stir in beans; cook over medium-high heat, stirring occasionally, 15 minutes. Remove from heat. Ladle chili into bowls; sprinkle with cheese and cilantro. 6 servings

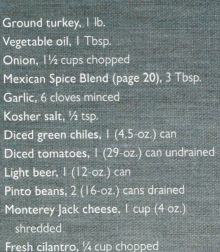

shallots + coriander + cumin + Fresh Salsa

"Using leftover turkey from Grilled Maple-Brined Turkey (page 148) makes these tacos an easy, delicious weeknight meal."

Turkey Tacos

1 Cook shallots in hot oil in a large saucepan over medium-high heat, stirring constantly, 1 minute. Add turkey, and cook, stirring often, 1 minute. Stir in broth, coriander, and cumin. Increase heat to high, and cook, stirring occasionally, 5 minutes or until liquid is almost completely absorbed. Stir in salt and pepper.

2 Heat tortillas according to package directions. Serve turkey mixture in tortillas with lettuce, queso fresco, and Fresh Salsa. 6 servings

Shallots, ⅓ cup finely chopped
Extra virgin olive oil, 2 Tbsp.
Shredded cooked turkey, 1 lb. (2¾ cups)
Chicken broth, 1 cup
Ground coriander, 1 tsp.
Ground cumin, 1 tsp.
Kosher salt, 1 tsp.
Freshly ground black pepper, ¾ tsp.
Flour tortillas, 12 (6-inch) soft taco-size
Lettuce, 1½ cups shredded
Queso fresco (fresh Mexican cheese),
  ¾ cup crumbled
Fresh Salsa

fresh salsa:

Tomatoes, 2 cups chopped
Fresh cilantro, 2 Tbsp. chopped
Fresh flat-leaf parsley, 2 Tbsp. chopped
Red onion, 2 Tbsp. chopped
Jalapeño pepper, 1½ Tbsp. seeded and chopped

Extra virgin olive oil, 2 Tbsp.
Fresh lime juice, 2 Tbsp.
Kosher salt, ½ tsp.
Freshly ground black pepper, ½ tsp.

1 Stir together all ingredients in a medium bowl. Cover and chill until ready to serve. Serve with a slotted spoon. 2 cups

drink: Mexican beer or margarita

"Look for semi-boneless quail at stores such as Whole Foods or order them from your butcher. This is such a pretty approach to Thanksgiving, but it's also a great party dish in general."

butter + celery + garlic + sage

Thanksgiving Quail with Cornbread-and-Sausage Stuffing

Cornbread or white country bread, 3 cups diced (about ¾-inch cubes)

Semi-boneless quail, 8 (about 1 lb. 5 oz.)

Unsalted butter, 6 Tbsp. softened and divided

Bulk pork sausage, 8 oz.

Onion, 1 medium finely diced

Celery, 2 ribs finely diced

Garlic, 2 cloves minced

Poultry seasoning, 2 tsp.

Chicken broth, 1 to 2 cups, divided

Fresh sage, 3 Tbsp. chopped

Kosher salt, 1 tsp., divided

Freshly ground black pepper, ½ tsp., divided

Wooden picks

Olive oil, 2 Tbsp.

Cranberry relish or chutney, 1 cup

Garnish: fresh sage leaves

1. Preheat oven to 350°. Bake cornbread in a single layer on a baking sheet 10 to 15 minutes or until toasted, stirring once halfway through. Remove from oven. Increase oven temperature to 450°.

2. Rinse quail, and pat dry.

3. Melt 2 Tbsp. butter in a large sauté pan over medium heat. Add sausage and next 3 ingredients, and cook, stirring constantly, 7 minutes or until sausage crumbles and is no longer pink and onion is translucent. If necessary, drain any drippings from pan. Stir in poultry seasoning. Stir in toasted cornbread, 1 cup broth, and chopped sage.

4. Cook, stirring often, over medium heat 3 minutes or until cornbread begins to break down. Stir in 2 Tbsp. butter. If mixture is dry, add up to 1 cup additional broth as needed. Season with ½ tsp. salt and ¼ tsp. pepper.

5. Pour cornbread mixture onto a baking sheet in an even layer. Cool 10 minutes.

6. Shape cornbread mixture into 8 (2-inch) balls. (Spoon remaining mixture into an 8-inch square baking dish, and bake at 450° for 20 minutes or until golden). Place 1 cornbread ball in cavity of each quail. Secure skin over breasts with wooden picks. Cross quail legs.

7. Fold 1 (12-inch-long, 4-inch-wide) piece of aluminum foil in half lengthwise twice to create a 12 x 1-inch strip. Curl foil into an oval just wide enough to hold quail. Repeat procedure, making 8 foil rings total. Place rings on a large, oven-proof sauté pan or roasting pan.

8. Cook quail, breast sides down, in 2 Tbsp. olive oil over medium-high heat 4 to 6 minutes or until brown, turning often. Transfer each quail to a foil ring,

placing legs down in ring. (Quail should be raised about an inch off the pan, allowing the fat to drip into pan.) Brush quail with remaining 2 Tbsp. butter, and sprinkle with remaining ½ tsp. salt and ¼ tsp. pepper. Bake quail at 450° for 18 minutes or until a meat thermometer inserted into thickest portion of breast registers 165°. Let stand 10 minutes.

9 Spoon 2 Tbsp. chutney onto each serving plate. Add quail. Serve with additional stuffing. Garnish, if desired. Serve immediately. 4 to 6 servings

Drink: Gamay Beaujolais

asparagus + Canadian bacon + eggs + Gruyère

Open-Faced Omelet with Asparagus and Canadian Bacon

1 Preheat broiler with oven rack 6 inches from heat. Snap off and discard tough ends of asparagus. Cut asparagus diagonally into ¼-inch pieces. Whisk together eggs, salt, and pepper in a bowl.

2 Heat oil in a 10-inch nonstick ovenproof skillet over medium heat, rotating pan to coat bottom evenly. Add bacon and asparagus, and cook, stirring occasionally, 2 to 4 minutes or until bacon is thoroughly heated and asparagus is crisp-tender.

3 Reduce heat to low, and add egg mixture. As egg mixture starts to cook, gently lift edges of omelet with a spatula, and tilt pan so uncooked portion flows underneath. Cook 2 minutes or until almost set.

4 Sprinkle with cheese. Broil 1 minute or until cheese is melted. Remove from oven, and carefully slide omelet onto a plate. Garnish, if desired. 1 serving

Open-Faced Omelet with Cottage Cheese Sauce: Process ½ cup small-curd cottage cheese and 1 Tbsp. milk in a blender until pureed. Spoon sauce over egg mixture in pan and prepare recipe as directed.

Open-Faced Omelet with Goat Cheese: Prepare recipe as directed, substituting goat cheese for Gruyère.

Open-Faced Omelet with Mushrooms, Onions, and Sausage: Omit asparagus and Canadian bacon. Prepare recipe as directed, cooking ⅓ cup chopped mushrooms, ¼ cup chopped onion, and ⅓ cup halved and sliced chicken sausage as directed in Step 2.

drink: Mimosa

"I love open-faced omelets or 'frittatas,' and this recipe is all-American. (Except for the 'Canadian' bacon!) Make it entirely out of egg whites to balance out the bacon, or use whole eggs. A well-seasoned pan like cast iron works nicely for this, because it acts like nonstick but is also ovenproof so it can be put under the broiler. My GreenPan™ cookware is also an ideal choice—it is nonstick and ovenproof. Promise me you will not put traditional nonstick cookware in your hot oven. It's not safe for your health or the life of the pan!"

Asparagus spears, 3
Large eggs, 3
Kosher salt, ⅛ tsp.
Freshly ground black pepper, ⅛ tsp.
Vegetable oil, 2 tsp.
Canadian bacon, ⅓ cup chopped
Gruyère cheese, 1 cup (4 oz.) shredded
Garnish: fresh basil leaves

"Family picnics always require deviled eggs—it's a Southern thing. This recipe marries my New England and Southern roots to make the perfect party food."

lemon juice + *mayonnaise* + *red onion* + *chives*

Deviled Eggs with Lobster

1 Place eggs in a single layer in a stainless-steel saucepan. (Do not use nonstick.) Add water to depth of 3 inches. Bring to a rolling boil; cover, remove from heat, and let stand 12 minutes.

2 Tap each egg firmly on the counter until cracks form all over the shell. Peel under cold running water.

3 Slice eggs in half lengthwise, and carefully remove yolks. Process yolks, lemon juice, and next 2 ingredients in a food processor just until blended. Fold in onion and next 5 ingredients. Spoon yolk mixture into egg white halves. Garnish, if desired. Serve immediately. 16 deviled eggs

*Fresh lump crabmeat, drained, may be substituted.

Note: I suggest using Hellmann's or Best Foods Mayonnaise.

Large eggs, 8
Fresh lemon juice, 2 Tbsp.
Mayonnaise, 2 Tbsp.
Sour cream, 1½ tsp.
Red onion, 1 Tbsp. finely diced
Fresh chives, 1 tsp. finely diced
Dry mustard, 1 tsp.
Kosher salt, ½ tsp.
Freshly ground black pepper, ¼ tsp.
Lobster tail meat, ½ cup cooked and
  finely diced*
Garnishes: paprika, finely diced red onion,
  chopped fresh chives, black sturgeon
  caviar

Drink: French Chardonnay/
  Pouilly-Fuissé

"Once you learn how to make my Semolina Polenta (page 122), you'll want to make it all the time! I love that it can be served any time of day, and it's really good with eggs for brunch. With a side of bacon or fresh fruit, coffee, and a newspaper, you have the perfect weekend breakfast.

I like to use fresh chives, flat-leaf parsley, and thyme in this recipe. You can also sprinkle some freshly grated Parmigiano-Reggiano or goat cheese over the ramekins when they come out of the oven."

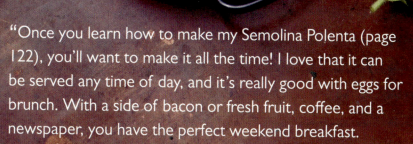

butter   +   eggs   +   assorted herbs

Baked Eggs in Semolina Polenta

1 Preheat oven to 350°. Lightly grease 4 ramekins using 2 Tbsp. softened butter. Place on a baking sheet. Spoon ½ cup Semolina Polenta into each ramekin, making a well in center of each.

2 Crack 1 egg into a small bowl; pour into a ramekin. Repeat procedure with remaining 3 eggs. Sprinkle with fresh herbs, salt, and pepper.

3 Bake at 350° for 15 to 20 minutes or until set. 4 servings

drink: Freshly brewed coffee or English breakfast tea

Unsalted butter, 2 Tbsp. softened
Semolina Polenta (page 122), 2 cups
Large eggs, 4
Assorted fresh herbs, 2 tsp. chopped
Kosher salt, ½ tsp.
Freshly ground black pepper, ½ tsp.

"What a perfect brunch item! Adding potatoes to the eggs stretches the eggs (thrifty, isn't it?), making the perfect deliciously inexpensive meal.

My aunt Maria Pia in Rome would make this frittata at breakfast, throw it in the cupboard, and then the kids would come home and eat it for lunch. It's great any time of day."

Bacon, ½ cup chopped
Baking potatoes, 2 cups peeled, diced, and cooked
White onion, 2 cups chopped
Garlic, 2 cloves minced
Celery, ½ cup minced
Large eggs, 12 lightly beaten
Kosher salt, 1 tsp.
Freshly ground black pepper, ½ tsp.
Smoked salmon, ¼ lb. thinly sliced
Avocado Salad

Drink: White Châteauneuf-du-Pape

bacon + garlic + celery + avocado

Potato Frittata with Avocado Salad and Smoked Salmon

1 Preheat oven to 350°. Cook bacon in a 12-inch ovenproof nonstick skillet over medium-high heat 6 to 8 minutes or until crisp; remove bacon, and drain on paper towels, reserving 1 Tbsp. drippings in skillet.

2 Sauté potatoes in hot drippings 5 minutes or until potatoes begin to brown. Add onion, garlic, and celery, and cook, stirring occasionally, 7 minutes or until tender. Remove from heat, and stir in bacon.

3 Whisk together eggs, salt, and pepper in a bowl. Pour egg mixture over vegetables in skillet.

4 Bake at 350° for 15 to 18 minutes or until set, removing halfway through cooking to gently lift edges of frittata with a spatula and tilting pan so uncooked portion flows underneath. Remove from oven, and let cool 2 minutes. Run a knife around edge of skillet to loosen, and invert onto a serving plate (see page 160). Cut into 8 wedges. Top each serving with smoked salmon and Avocado Salad. 8 servings

avocado salad:

Sour cream, ¼ cup
Fresh chives, 2 Tbsp. chopped
Ripe avocados, 2 peeled and diced
Extra virgin olive oil, 2 Tbsp.

Fresh lime juice, 2 Tbsp.
Kosher salt, ¼ tsp.
Freshly ground black pepper, 1 dash

1 Toss together all ingredients until blended. Serve immediately. 1½ cups

"The Italian version of an omelet, a frittata is delicious on its own, but shrimp, oh the shrimp…it just takes it over the top. I suggest using 1 tablespoon each of chives, mint, oregano, and parsley for the assorted herbs. I adore those four combined, but choose whatever suits your taste."

Asparagus spears, 3
Unpeeled jumbo raw shrimp,
   10 (16/20 count)
Large eggs, 8
Assorted fresh herbs, 4 Tbsp. chopped
Kosher salt, ¾ tsp.
Freshly ground black pepper, ¼ tsp.
Unsalted butter, 2 Tbsp.
Extra virgin olive oil, 3 Tbsp., divided
Feta cheese, ⅓ cup crumbled
Garlic, 2 cloves chopped
Plum tomatoes, ¼ cup chopped
Fresh lemon juice, 2 Tbsp.
Kosher salt, ⅛ tsp.
Freshly ground black pepper, ⅛ tsp.
My Favorite Pesto (page 28)

Drink: South African Chardonnay

assorted herbs + feta + asparagus + My Favorite Pesto

Shrimp Frittata with My Favorite Pesto

1 Preheat broiler with oven rack 4 inches from heat. Snap off and discard tough ends of asparagus. Cut asparagus diagonally into ½-inch pieces. Peel shrimp; devein, if desired. Whisk together eggs and next 3 ingredients in a bowl. Stir in asparagus.

2 Melt butter with 1 Tbsp. oil in a 12-inch nonstick ovenproof skillet over medium-high heat. Add egg mixture, reduce heat to medium low, and sprinkle with feta cheese. Cover and cook 6 to 8 minutes or until edges are cooked, removing cover halfway through cooking to gently lift edges of frittata with a spatula and tilting pan so uncooked portion flows underneath.

3 Meanwhile, cook shrimp in remaining 2 Tbsp. hot oil in a medium-size nonstick skillet over medium heat 3 minutes or just until shrimp turn pink. Add garlic, and cook, stirring constantly, 1 minute. Remove from heat, and stir in tomatoes, lemon juice, and ⅛ tsp. each salt and pepper.

4 Uncover frittata, and broil 2 minutes or until browned and set. Remove from oven, and run a knife around edge of skillet to loosen. Invert onto a serving plate. Top frittata with shrimp mixture. Serve with My Favorite Pesto. 4 to 6 servings

frittata (fri-TAH-tuh) n. from the Italian "fritto" meaning fried, this unfolded omelet resembles a large pancake.

Meats

In this chapter I provide flavorful recipes that utilize an array of different cuts of meat. But it's just the tip of the iceberg, because the cuts available to the home cook are many.

There are a few rules of thumb when cooking meat. Tougher cuts of meat are those closer to the hoof or the mouth of the animal and taste best when slowly braised until they become meltingly tender. Cuts closer to the back and middle of the animal are more tender and marbled with fat, so they benefit from quick-cooking methods like grilling or pan searing. Butchers love talking about this stuff, so get to know yours and ask questions. Then get cooking!

filet mignon (fil-AY min-YON)

n. literally "dainty fillet," this is a thick slice or medallion cut from the beef tenderloin.

166

shallots + green peppercorns + cognac + cream

Filet Mignon au Poivre

1 Preheat oven to 425°. Let beef stand at room temperature 15 to 30 minutes. Sprinkle with ½ tsp. salt and pepper.

2 Cook steaks in 1 Tbsp. hot olive oil in an ovenproof skillet over medium-high heat 3 minutes on each side or until browned.

3 Bake at 425° for 7 minutes or until a meat thermometer inserted into thickest portion registers 145° (medium-rare). Transfer to a serving plate, reserving any accumulated juices, and let stand 10 minutes.

4 While the steaks stand, wipe skillet clean. Melt butter with remaining 1 Tbsp. olive oil in skillet over medium heat. Add shallots, remaining ½ tsp. salt, and peppercorns, and cook, stirring occasionally, 5 minutes or until shallots are soft and peppercorns are fragrant.

5 Remove skillet from heat; stir in cognac, and carefully ignite the fumes above mixture with a long match or long multipurpose lighter. Let flames die down.

6 Return to heat. Cook, stirring often, until liquid is almost completely evaporated (about 1 minute). Add cream and reserved juices, and cook, stirring often, 4 to 5 minutes or until thickened. Pour through a wire-mesh strainer into a bowl. Return 2 Tbsp. shallots and peppercorns to sauce; discard remaining solids. Serve steaks with sauce. 4 servings

Drink: French Cabernet Sauvignon

"A classic steakhouse preparation, this is indulgent and definitely special-occasion fare. Filet mignon is the perfect cut for a luxurious sauce. Sear the meat over high heat to develop a nice crust, and then finish it off quickly in the oven. Green peppercorns are milder in flavor than mature black peppercorns and a subtle choice with the cognac and fresh cream in the sauce. Make sure to have all your ingredients prepped and ready to throw in the pan before you start cooking. Then focus on the sauce while the steaks rest, and this elegant dinner will come together in minutes."

Beef tenderloin fillets, 4 (6- to 8-oz.) trimmed
Kosher salt, 1 tsp., divided
Freshly ground black pepper, ½ tsp.
Extra virgin olive oil, 2 Tbsp., divided
Unsalted butter, 1 Tbsp.
Shallots, 3 minced (about ½ cup)
Green peppercorns, ½ cup
Cognac, ½ cup
Heavy cream, 1 cup

"I love cooking beef on the bone because it releases lots of flavor. This is a simple preparation that can be served on its own with just a grinding of my Rosemary and Lemon Salt (page 15) over the top or paired with one of the three amazing sauces included below and on the next page."

Classic T-Bone

T-bone steak, 1 (about 1½ to 2 lb.)   **Kosher salt and freshly ground black pepper**

❶ Season steak with desired amount of salt and pepper. Cook steak in a lightly greased grill pan over medium-high heat 10 minutes on each side or to desired degree of doneness. Let stand 5 minutes before serving. 2 servings

T-1 Sauce

Anchovy fillets in oil, 6 drained
Garlic, 3 cloves minced
Olive oil, 2 Tbsp.
Capers, 2 Tbsp. drained, rinsed, and patted dry

Orange juice, ½ cup
Prune juice, ½ cup
Dijon mustard, 2 Tbsp.
Tomato paste, 2 Tbsp.

❶ Cook anchovies and garlic in hot oil in a medium saucepan over medium-low heat, stirring often, 4 minutes or until garlic is lightly browned, smashing anchovies as they cook. Add capers, and cook 1 minute. Add remaining ingredients, and increase heat to high. Bring to a boil. Reduce heat to low, and simmer, stirring occasionally, 10 minutes. Remove from heat, and let cool completely (about 30 minutes).

❷ Process anchovy mixture in a blender until pureed. 1 cup

Cognac-Peppercorn Sauce

Unsalted butter, 1 Tbsp.
Vegetable oil, 1 Tbsp.
Shallots, 3 minced
Green peppercorns, ⅓ cup
Cognac, ½ cup
Heavy cream, 1 cup
Kosher salt, ½ tsp.

❶ Melt butter with oil in a sauté pan over medium heat; add shallots and peppercorns, and cook, stirring often, 5 minutes. Remove pan from heat; stir in cognac, and carefully ignite the fumes just above mixture with a long match or long multipurpose lighter. Let flames die down.

❷ Return to heat. Cook over medium heat until liquid is reduced to about 1 Tbsp. (about 30 seconds to 1 minute). Add cream and salt, and cook, stirring often, 7 to 8 minutes or until thickened. Pour through a wire-mesh strainer into a bowl. Return 2 Tbsp. peppercorns to sauce; discard remaining solids. ⅔ cup

L.A.-Style Sauce

Cubanelle or sweet green Italian peppers, 2 seeded and coarsely chopped
Ancho chile powder, 3 Tbsp.
Vegetable oil, 2 Tbsp.
Honey, 2 Tbsp.
Soy sauce, 1 Tbsp.
Worcestershire sauce, 2 Tbsp.

❶ Sauté peppers and ancho chile powder in hot oil in a medium saucepan over medium heat 8 minutes.

❷ Transfer peppers to a food processor. Add honey, soy sauce, and Worcestershire sauce. Pulse 5 times or until blended. With processor running, pour about ¼ cup water through food chute in a slow, steady stream, processing until smooth and desired consistency. 1 cup

drink: Meritage/California Red Blend

"Sliders seem to be all the rage. The burger recipe on its own is simple and great, but the Crispy Fried Onions and my Mustard Relish variations take it over the top."

red onions + Cheddar + Mustard Relish

Game Day Sliders

Crispy Fried Onions
Canola oil
Red onions, 2 large thinly sliced

Sliders
Ground round, 1½ lb.
Kosher salt, 1 tsp.
Freshly ground black pepper, ½ tsp.
Cheddar cheese slices, 3 (0.73-oz.) quartered
Slider buns, 12
Mustard Relish (page 25), ½ cup
Tomato, 1 sliced
Romaine lettuce leaves, 4 shredded
Ketchup
Mayonnaise

1 Prepare onions: Pour oil to a depth of 2 inches into a large deep skillet; heat over medium-high heat to 350°. Fry onion slices, in batches, 2 to 3 minutes or until golden and crisp. Drain.

2 Prepare sliders: Preheat grill to 350° to 400° (medium-high) heat. Combine ground beef, salt, and pepper in a large bowl until blended. (Do not overwork meat mixture.)

3 Shape meat mixture into 12 (2-inch) patties. Grill patties, covered with grill lid, 4 minutes on each side or until beef is no longer pink in center; place 1 cheese quarter on each patty.

4 Grill buns, cut sides down, covered with grill lid, 1 minute or until toasted. Spread about 2 tsp. Mustard Relish on bottom of each bun. Top each with 1 beef patty, an equal amount of Crispy Fried Onions, 1 tomato slice, and 2 Tbsp. lettuce. Spread bun tops with ketchup and mayonnaise. Cover sliders with bun tops. 4 servings

Drink: American brown ale

"This ingredient list might look daunting, but I promise each item adds loads of flavor. After baking, let the meatballs simmer slowly in my Quick and Luscious Tomato Sauce (page 31) for an hour to soak up more flavor. If you don't want to buy three types of meat, use equal parts ground chuck and pork butt."

onion + parsley + Todd's Spiced Ketchup + Roasted Tomatoes

Mozzarella-Stuffed Meatballs with Roasted Tomatoes

1. Prepare meatballs: Preheat oven to 375°. Cook onion and garlic in 3 Tbsp. hot oil in a medium-size sauté pan over medium-high heat, stirring often, 7 minutes or until softened. Transfer to a large bowl. Let cool completely (about 30 minutes).

2. Add veal, next 9 ingredients, and 1 cup Parmigiano-Reggiano cheese to onion mixture in bowl. Combine, using hands. Shape mixture into 20 (2-inch) balls, shaping each meatball around 1 mozzarella cube. Place stuffed meatballs on a lightly greased rack in a broiler pan.

3. Bake at 375° for 25 minutes or until meat is no longer pink. Remove from oven. Increase oven temperature to 500°.

4. Prepare tomatoes: Toss together tomatoes and next 2 ingredients in a bowl. Spread tomatoes in a single layer on a baking sheet.

5. Bake at 500° for 15 minutes or until blistered.

6. Transfer meatballs to a serving bowl. Top with tomatoes. Sprinkle with remaining ½ cup Parmigiano-Reggiano cheese. 4 servings

Drink: Chianti Classico

Meatballs

Onion, 1 cup chopped
Garlic, 4 cloves chopped
Olive oil, 3 Tbsp.
Ground veal, ¾ lb.
Ground chuck, ¾ lb.
Ground pork shoulder roast (Boston butt), ¾ lb.
Soft, fresh breadcrumbs, 3 cups
Fresh flat-leaf parsley, ½ cup chopped
Todd's Spiced Ketchup (page 24) or store-bought ketchup, ¼ cup
Large eggs, 2
Dried oregano, 2 Tbsp.
Kosher salt, 1 tsp.
Freshly ground black pepper, ½ tsp.
Parmigiano-Reggiano cheese, 1½ cups freshly grated, divided
Fresh mozzarella cheese, 4 oz. cut into 20 (1-inch) cubes

Roasted Tomatoes

Cherry tomatoes, 2 qt.
Olive oil, ¼ cup
Kosher salt, 1 tsp.

"Short ribs are a favorite, but everyone always braises them the same way—with tomatoes, red wine, or beef stock. One day I got the bright idea to use tequila as the braising liquid. You have to trust me on this one—it creates a depth of flavor that is indescribable but subtle. Serve over Semolina Polenta (page 122), use as a substitute for the prime rib in my Prime Rib Chili (page 174), or shred the meat for tacos. Don't forget to serve some really good tequila alongside!"

Dark tequila + jalapeño peppers + cilantro + bay leaves

Beef short ribs, 4 lb.
Kosher salt, I Tbsp.
Freshly ground black pepper, I Tbsp.
Olive oil, 2 Tbsp.
Dark tequila, 3 cups
Carrots, 2 cups diced
Yellow onion, 2 cups diced
Celery ribs, I cup diced
Jalapeño peppers, 3 halved
Fresh cilantro sprigs, 10
Fresh thyme sprigs, 3
Bay leaves, 3
Black peppercorns, I Tbsp.
Beef broth, 6 cups

Tequila-Braised Short Ribs

1 Preheat oven to 400°. Sprinkle ribs with salt and pepper. Cook ribs, in batches, in hot oil in a large Dutch oven over medium-high heat 2 to 3 minutes on each side or until browned. Remove from heat. Remove ribs from Dutch oven; drain.

2 Add tequila to Dutch oven, stirring to loosen particles from bottom of pan. Add carrots and next 7 ingredients; add ribs and broth, and cover.

3 Bake at 400° for 2 to 3 hours or until meat is tender enough to fall off the bone. 4 servings

Drink: Tequila shots or an American Grenache, Syrah, or Mourvèdre Blend

"Short ribs are one of the most pleasing and satisfying cuts of meat when prepared well. And this Korean marinade is insane! Asian pear is the secret ingredient that Koreans use regularly in marinades."

Asian pear   +   soy sauce   +   ginger   +   Dark sesame oil

Seoul Short Ribs

1 Grate pear using large holes of a box grater (about 1 cup grated). Whisk together pear, soy sauce, and next 6 ingredients in a large shallow dish or large zip-top plastic freezer bag; add ribs. Cover or seal, and chill 12 to 24 hours.

2 Preheat oven to 350°. Remove ribs from marinade, reserving marinade. Cook ribs, in batches, in hot oil in a large Dutch oven over medium-high heat 2 to 3 minutes on each side or until browned. Remove from heat, and remove ribs from Dutch oven; drain any accumulated liquid.

3 Add broth and reserved marinade to Dutch oven, scraping to loosen particles from bottom of Dutch oven. Return ribs to Dutch oven. Bring to a boil.

4 Bake, covered, at 350° for 2½ to 3 hours or until meat is tender enough to fall off the bone. Transfer ribs to a serving platter. Garnish, if desired. 4 servings

Drink: California Zinfandel

Asian pear, 1
Soy sauce, 2 cups
Sweet rice wine, ¼ cup
Fresh ginger, 3 Tbsp. chopped
Sugar, 2 Tbsp.
Sriracha sauce, 2 Tbsp.
Dark sesame oil, 2 Tbsp.
Garlic, 3 cloves chopped
Beef short ribs, 3 lb.
Vegetable oil, 1 Tbsp.
Beef broth, 1 (32-oz.) container
Garnishes: toasted sesame seeds, chopped fresh cilantro, thinly sliced green onions

"If there were a 'celebrity' chili, this would be it. Prime rib is such an unexpected cut to use in chili, but it's luxurious. A heaping bowl of this served with my Pear Cider (page 43) is football party food at its finest."

red onion + Anaheim chiles + Mexican Spice Blend + Monterey Jack

Prime Rib Chili

Prime rib steak, 2 lb. cut into ½-inch cubes
Kosher salt, ¼ tsp.
Freshly ground black pepper, ⅛ tsp.
Olive oil, ¼ cup
Red onion, 1 large finely diced
Garlic, 4 cloves finely chopped
Anaheim chiles, 2 seeded and diced
Mexican Spice Blend (page 20), 2 to 4 Tbsp.
Low-sodium chicken broth, 5 cups
Chopped tomatoes, 1 (14.5-oz.) can
Assorted canned beans, 2 cups drained and rinsed
Fresh lime juice, 2 Tbsp.
Monterey Jack cheese, 2 cups (8 oz.) shredded

❶ Sprinkle steak with salt and pepper. Cook, in batches, in hot oil in a large Dutch oven over high heat, stirring occasionally, 4 minutes or until browned on all sides. Transfer to a bowl, reserving drippings in Dutch oven.

❷ Reduce heat to medium. Add onion to hot drippings, and cook, stirring often, 5 minutes. Add garlic, and cook 2 minutes. Stir in chiles and Mexican Spice Blend, and cook, stirring often, 2 minutes. Return steak to Dutch oven. Add broth and tomatoes.

❸ Bring to a simmer. Cover, reduce heat to medium, and simmer, stirring occasionally, 45 minutes. Stir in beans, and cook 15 minutes. Remove from heat, and stir in lime juice. Serve with cheese. 6 cups

Drink: Pear Cider (page 43)

"While in Crete, I was determined to find the quintessential Greek restaurant serving authentic Greek food, not a touristy version of it. I wanted a Greek momma in the kitchen as insurance. So one day, while driving aimlessly through the hills overlooking the ocean, we stopped for a late lunch. We walked into a tiny restaurant with an open kitchen that was cranking out feta and tomato salads, grilled squid, and lamb chops like these. The 'momma' poured fresh lemon juice and olive oil over the top of the lamb to serve. I got the meal I was looking for!"

rosemary + olive oil + lemons

Greek Island Lamb Chops

1 Preheat oven to 350°. Arrange rosemary sprigs in a single layer in a broiler pan. Sprinkle lamb with salt and pepper.

2 Cook chops, in batches, in 1 Tbsp. hot oil (per batch) in a large sauté pan over medium-high heat 1 to 2 minutes on each side or until golden brown. Transfer chops and any accumulated juices to prepared pan.

3 Bake at 350° for 8 to 10 minutes (medium-rare) or to desired degree of doneness. Let stand 10 minutes. Transfer chops to a serving dish, and squeeze juice from lemons over chops. Serve with Orzo with Feta Cheese and Mint. Garnish, if desired. 6 servings

Fresh rosemary sprigs, 8
Lamb loin chops, 12 (6-oz.)
Kosher salt, 1 tsp.
Freshly ground black pepper, 1 tsp.
Extra virgin olive oil, 2 Tbsp.
Lemons, 2 halved
Orzo with Feta Cheese and Mint (page 120)
Garnish: fresh rosemary sprig

Drink: Washington Merlot

"Lamb is so delicious on its own, and the simple rub of rosemary, garlic, lemon zest, and fennel seeds is the perfect complement to the chops. This recipe is fast and totally impressive. Pickled cherry peppers and a bit of their juice add an explosion of mouth-watering flavor."

Lamb rib chops, 12 (about 2 lb.)
Kosher salt, ½ tsp.
Freshly ground black pepper, ½ tsp.
Fresh rosemary, 2 Tbsp. chopped
Lemon zest, 1 Tbsp.
Garlic, 3 cloves coarsely chopped
Fennel seeds, 1 Tbsp.
Extra virgin olive oil, 3 Tbsp., divided
Jarred sweet cherry peppers, 8 stemmed and coarsely chopped
Shallots, 2 Tbsp. thinly sliced
Juice from jar of cherry peppers, 3 Tbsp.
Fresh flat-leaf parsley, 3 Tbsp. chopped

Drink: Italian Brunello di Montalcino

Lamb Lollipops with Cherry Peppers

❶ Place 1 chop between 2 sheets of plastic wrap, and flatten to ½-inch thickness, holding the bone while you pound and using a rolling pin or flat side of a meat mallet. Repeat procedure with remaining chops. Place chops in a 13- x 9-inch baking dish. Sprinkle with salt and pepper.

❷ Crush together rosemary, next 3 ingredients, and 1 Tbsp. oil using a mortar and pestle. Stir in 1 Tbsp. oil. Spread paste over chops. Cover and let stand at room temperature 30 minutes or chill up to 3 hours.

❸ Cook chops, in 2 batches, in 1½ tsp. hot oil (per batch) in a large skillet over medium-high heat 2 to 3 minutes on each side (medium-rare) or to desired degree of doneness. Transfer to a serving dish.

❹ Add peppers and shallots to hot drippings in skillet, and sauté 1 minute. Add juice from peppers, and cook 1 minute. Pour sauce over chops, and sprinkle with parsley. Serve immediately. 4 servings

lime + Aleppo pepper + rosemary + red onion

Lamb Shish Kabobs with Wild Mushroom Couscous

❶ Grate zest and squeeze juice from limes. Whisk together zest, juice, wine, and next 5 ingredients in a large shallow dish or zip-top plastic freezer bag; add lamb, onion, and bell peppers. Cover or seal, and chill 6 to 8 hours.

❷ Soak wooden skewers in water 30 minutes. Lightly grease grill; preheat to 350° to 400° (medium-high) heat.

❸ Remove lamb and vegetables from marinade, discarding marinade. Thread lamb, onion, and bell peppers alternately onto skewers, leaving a ¼-inch space between pieces. Grill kabobs, covered with grill lid, 2 minutes on each side or until lamb is cooked to desired degree of doneness and vegetables are crisp-tender. Serve with Wild Mushroom Couscous. 12 servings

Drink: Australian Shiraz

"I love pretty much all cuts of lamb, but leg of lamb is uncommonly delicious, and this is a really quick way to cook it. Mediterranean countries do lamb best—they understand the bold flavors that marry well with the meat's distinctiveness. My addition of Aleppo pepper is a standout."

Limes, 2
Dry white wine, ½ cup
Olive oil, ¼ cup
Aleppo pepper, 4 tsp.
Fresh rosemary, 1 Tbsp. chopped
Kosher salt, 1 tsp.
Freshly ground black pepper, ½ tsp.
Lamb sirloin, 2 lb. cut into 1-inch cubes
Red onion, 1 large cut into 1-inch cubes
Red bell pepper, 1 large cut into 1-inch cubes
Green bell pepper, 1 large cut into 1-inch cubes
Wooden skewers, 12 (12-inch)
Wild Mushroom Couscous (page 119)

navel oranges + cinnamon + cumin + coriander

North African Lamb Shanks

❶ Preheat oven to 400°. Season lamb with salt and pepper. Cook lamb in hot oil in a 12-inch cast-iron skillet or sauté pan over medium-high heat 8 to 10 minutes or until browned; drain. Transfer lamb to a roasting pan.

❷ Discard oil and drippings. Add onions and next 2 ingredients to skillet, and sauté 2 to 3 minutes. Stir in oranges and next 3 ingredients, and cook, stirring occasionally, 5 minutes or until onions are softened and spices are fragrant. Increase heat to high, and stir in orange juice. Cook, stirring occasionally, 10 minutes or until liquid is reduced by half. Stir in broth, and cook, stirring occasionally, 10 minutes. Pour vegetable mixture over lamb in roasting pan. Cover tightly.

❸ Bake at 400° for 3 hours or until meat is tender enough to fall off the bone. Let stand 5 minutes before serving. 4 servings .

"When traveling through North Africa, I always try to indulge in lamb shanks. They're full of flavor, and they pair nicely with the local couscous. Don't be surprised—the entire orange, peel and all, goes into this sauce."

Bone-in lamb shanks, 4 (about 5 lb.)
Kosher salt, 1½ tsp.
Freshly ground black pepper, 1½ tsp.
Olive oil, ¼ cup
Yellow onions, 4 cups coarsely chopped
Celery ribs, 2 coarsely chopped
Carrot, 1 coarsely chopped
Navel oranges, 2 coarsely chopped
Cinnamon sticks, 4
Cumin seeds, 2 Tbsp.
Coriander seeds, 2 Tbsp.
Orange juice, 2 cups
Chicken broth, 4 cups

Drink: Argentinian Malbec

Technique: Braising makes tough, inexpensive cuts tender and incredibly flavorful. Caramelization created by searing the meat before braising is a great way to add more flavor. Make sure your pan is very hot and there is a thin layer of oil in the bottom of the pan before adding the meat. Allow plenty of time for the outside to develop a brown crust before flipping the meat. A final long, slow simmer cooks the meat through until it falls off the bone when it's done.

"The incredible 'crust' on this pork chop is really a simple compound butter I put on top for the last two minutes of cooking. My maple brine for turkey (page 148) is delicious with these pork chops, too. It infuses both moisture and flavor into lean meat. Serve this with a side of sautéed spinach with lemon and butter and my Creamy Miso Sweet Potatoes (page 112)."

maple syrup   blue cheese   almonds

Double-Cut Pork Chops with Blue Cheese–Almond "Crust"

Bone-in (double-cut) pork loin chops, 4
  (1½ lb., each 2 inches thick)
maple brine (page 148)
Blue Cheese–Almond Butter (page 18)
Olive oil, 2 Tbsp.
Garnish: lemon wedges

Drink: Provence Rosé

1 Place chops and brine in a 12-qt. stainless-steel stockpot. Cover and chill 24 hours.

2 Place ¼ cup Blue Cheese–Almond Butter between 2 sheets of plastic wrap; flatten to equal width and shape as a chop. Repeat procedure with remaining butter, forming 4 discs. Wrap in plastic wrap, and freeze.

3 Preheat oven to 375°. Remove chops from brine, discarding brine. Rinse chops, and pat dry. Let stand at room temperature 15 to 30 minutes.

4 Cook chops in hot oil in a large cast-iron skillet over medium-high heat 15 minutes or until browned on all sides.

5 Bake at 375° for 7 minutes or until a meat thermometer inserted into the thickest portion of chop registers 140°. Remove from oven, and let stand 5 minutes. Increase oven temperature to broil with oven rack 3 inches from heat.

6 Top each chop with 1 butter disc. Broil chops 2 to 3 minutes or until butter begins to bubble and turns lightly brown. Garnish, if desired. Serve immediately. 4 servings

"Let me demystify pork butt for you…this cut is actually 'shoulder.' Whatever you call it, it's a versatile cut that begs to be slow cooked. Sprinkle my Berbere Spice Blend (page 21) over it, try it with Mexican spices, or use this recipe that is full of some of my favorite flavors: rosemary, garlic, and citrus zest. For pulled pork sandwiches, pair the meat with my Barbecue Sauce (page 24) or shred it for tacos."

rosemary   +   orange zest   +   lemon zest   +   garlic

Slow-Roasted Pork

1 Trim excess fat from pork. Rinse pork, and pat dry with paper towels. Stir together 3 Tbsp. oil, rosemary, and next 5 ingredients; spread on all sides of pork. Place pork in a large shallow dish or large zip-top plastic freezer bag. Cover or seal, and chill at least 8 hours.

2 Preheat oven to 350°. Pour remaining 3 Tbsp. oil into a Dutch oven. Add pork. Cover and bake at 350° for 3 hours and 45 minutes or until fork tender, basting twice with pan juices. Let stand until cool enough to handle. Shred pork using fingers or 2 forks. 6 to 8 servings

Bone-in pork shoulder roast (Boston butt), 1 (6-lb.)
Olive oil, 6 Tbsp., divided
Fresh rosemary, 2 Tbsp. finely chopped
Kosher salt, 2 tsp.
Freshly ground black pepper, 1 tsp.
Orange zest, 1 Tbsp.
Lemon zest, 2 tsp.
Garlic cloves, 4 minced

Drink: German bock beer

Fish and Shellfish

With the environmental issues affecting the fishing industry, getting to know your fishmonger is imperative. Shopping for fish can be intimidating—having to know when to choose farm-raised fish, buy frozen, opt for fresh local catches, or what overfished varieties should be avoided. Seek out a fish purveyor you trust, because the rules are constantly changing, and there are different variables to consider for each type of fish or seafood you're purchasing. Show your fishmonger you take care when making your selection. Fish should always smell fresh like the sea, so don't hesitate to smell it. (If that's frowned upon, you're in the wrong place.) When buying whole fish, look for bright red gills and clear eyes. When buying sushi-grade fish, don't be afraid to ask your fishmonger to go to the back and pull out the freshest piece he has. He should always be willing to tell you how long a piece has been sitting in the case. Once you find someone you can trust, become a regular customer. You'll be treated to the best cuts and will develop a relationship from which you can learn a lot.

"To say I'm fish taco–obsessed would be an understatement. It's the combination of textures and flavors that I love—flaky fried fish, crunchy cabbage, and creamy avocado—all tied together with the herbal bite of my Chimichurri (page 28). You certainly don't need to use all three of the sauces all the time, but each one adds a little spike of welcome flavor. If frying is not your thing, grill the fish fillets brushed with olive oil and seasoned with a bit of salt and pepper, and then break them up into chunks to build your tacos!"

Fried Fish Tacos

Semolina or pasta flour, ½ cup
All-purpose flour, ½ cup
Kosher salt, ½ tsp.
Freshly ground black pepper, ¼ tsp.
Fresh snapper fillets, about 1 lb. skinned
Vegetable oil
Flour tortillas, 8 (6-inch) fajita-size
Caper Tartar Sauce (page 25), ½ cup
Napa cabbage, 1 cup finely shredded
Avocado Crema (page 29), ½ cup*
Chimichurri (page 28), ½ cup

Drink: Light lager or Mexican beer

❶ Stir together first 4 ingredients in a shallow dish. Dredge fish in flour mixture, shaking off excess.

❷ Pour oil to a depth of 2 inches into a large Dutch oven; heat over medium heat to 350°. Fry fish, in batches, 1½ to 3 minutes on each side or until golden brown and fish flakes with a fork. Drain on a paper towel–lined plate. Keep warm.

❸ Heat tortillas, in batches, in a large nonstick skillet over medium heat 2 to 3 minutes on each side or until lightly toasted and thoroughly heated. Remove from heat.

❹ Top each tortilla with 1 Tbsp. Caper Tartar Sauce. Break fish into pieces; top tortillas with fish and cabbage. Dollop with Avocado Crema, and drizzle with Chimichurri. 4 servings

*Sour cream may be substituted.

"Tuna Tartare will never go out of style if it's prepared right. The fresh herbs mixed with the raw tuna and the deep flavors of the sesame oil are a powerful combination. This fish taco is truly unforgettable."

 +  +  +

green onions   mixed herbs   ginger   Vietnamese chile paste

Tuna Tartare Tacos

1 Stir together first 10 ingredients in a large shallow dish or zip-top plastic freezer bag; add fish, turning to coat. Cover or seal 20 minutes to 1 hour.

2 Heat tortillas, in batches, in a large nonstick skillet over medium heat 2 to 3 minutes on each side or until lightly toasted and thoroughly heated. Remove from heat.

3 Remove fish from marinade, discarding marinade. Top tortillas with fish. Dollop with Avocado Crema. Serve immediately. 8 servings

*Sour cream may be substituted.

Note: People at risk for foodborne illness should avoid eating raw fish.

Green onions, 4 finely chopped
Fresh basil, 1 Tbsp. chopped
Fresh cilantro, 1 Tbsp. chopped
Fresh mint, 1 Tbsp. chopped
Fresh ginger, 1 Tbsp. finely chopped
Extra virgin olive oil, 2 Tbsp.
Vietnamese chile paste, 2 tsp.
Toasted sesame oil, 1 tsp.
Kosher salt, 1 tsp.
Freshly ground black pepper, ½ tsp.
Sushi-grade tuna, 1½ lb. cut into ¼-inch pieces
Flour tortillas, 8 (6-inch) fajita-size
Avocado Crema, ½ cup (page 29)*

Drink: Light lager or Mexican beer

"This is a classic Olives restaurant recipe: a combination of Mediterranean flavors with my favorite tuna. When buying tuna, look for bright, freshly colored fish that smells like the sea. Make sure your pan is very hot so you get a beautiful seared crust while leaving the fish rare in the middle."

Kalamata olives   +   shallots   +   rosemary   +   capers

Pan-Seared Tuna with Olive Vinaigrette and Roasted Tomatoes

Kalamata olives, ½ cup pitted and chopped
Extra virgin olive oil, ½ cup
Fresh lemon juice, 2 Tbsp.
Shallots, 2 tsp. chopped
Fresh rosemary, 2 tsp. chopped
Fresh flat-leaf parsley, 2 tsp. chopped
Anchovy fillets, 1 tsp. chopped
Capers, 1 tsp. drained and chopped
Kosher salt, 1 tsp., divided
Sushi-grade tuna loin, 1¼ lb.
Freshly ground black pepper, ½ tsp.
Extra virgin olive oil, 1 Tbsp.
Roasted Tomatoes, 8 halved (page 30)

❶ Stir together first 8 ingredients and ½ tsp. salt in a bowl until well blended.

❷ Sprinkle fish with pepper and remaining ½ tsp. salt. Cook in 1 Tbsp. hot oil in a heavy sauté pan over high heat 1 minute on each side (rare) or to desired degree of doneness. Transfer fish to a plate, and let stand 3 minutes. Cut into 4 equal pieces.

❸ Divide Roasted Tomatoes among 4 individual serving plates. Top with fish, and drizzle with desired amount of vinaigrette. Reserve any remaining vinaigrette for another use. 4 servings

Note: Vinaigrette may be made up to 1 day ahead and chilled until ready to serve. Serve at room temperature.

Drink: Oregon Pinot Noir

"There's something about this combination that is magical. I think it's the blend of spices on the fish that pairs perfectly with the crunchy, creamy yogurt sauce. Ask your fishmonger to recommend the best salmon. They'll have different opinions, depending on where you live!"

Za'atar Spice Blend   garlic   black pepper

Grilled Moroccan-Spiced Salmon with Cucumber-Yogurt Sauce

Salmon fillets, 4 (6-oz.) skin on
Olive oil, 3 Tbsp.
Za'atar Spice Blend (page 21), 2 Tbsp.
Kosher salt, ¼ tsp.
Freshly ground black pepper, ⅛ tsp.
Cucumber-Yogurt Sauce
Fettoush (page 70)

Drink: Spanish Tempranillo

1 Preheat grill to 350° to 400° (medium-high) heat. Brush fish with oil, and sprinkle with next 3 ingredients. Grill, covered with grill lid, 3 minutes on each side (medium-rare) or to desired degree of doneness. Serve with Cucumber-Yogurt Sauce and Fettoush. 4 servings

Note: Za'atar is a Middle Eastern spice blend that can be found in most Middle Eastern markets.

cucumber-yogurt sauce:

English cucumber, ⅔ cup chopped
Plain yogurt, ½ cup
Fresh flat-leaf parsley leaves, ¼ cup
Fresh cilantro leaves, ¼ cup
Jalapeño pepper, 2 tsp. seeded and chopped

Garlic clove, 1 small chopped
Kosher salt, ⅓ tsp.
Freshly ground black pepper, ¼ tsp.

1 Process all ingredients in a blender until smooth. 1 ¼ cups

"Think of chermoula as Moroccan chimichurri, with cilantro and garlic as the star ingredients. The combination is clean and herbal. Once you taste it, you'll want to put it on everything."

cilantro + garlic + paprika + cumin

Chermoula Shrimp

1 Peel shrimp; devein, if desired.

2 Pulse cilantro and next 4 ingredients in a food processor or blender 5 times or until coarsely chopped. With processor running, pour oil and lemon juice through food chute in a slow, steady stream, processing until smooth. Reserve some for dipping.

3 Combine shrimp and cilantro mixture in a large shallow dish or zip-top plastic freezer bag; cover or seal, and chill 30 minutes to 4 hours.

4 Soak wooden skewers in water 30 minutes.

5 Coat cold cooking grate of grill with cooking spray, and place on grill. Preheat grill to 350° to 400° (medium-high) heat. Remove shrimp from marinade, discarding marinade. Thread 3 shrimp lengthwise onto each skewer. Sprinkle with salt.

6 Place shrimp skewers on cooking grate of grill, and grill, covered with grill lid, 2 to 3 minutes on each side or just until shrimp turn pink. 6 servings

Unpeeled large raw shrimp, 3 dozen (31/35 count)

Fresh cilantro leaves, 1 cup loosely packed

Garlic, 4 cloves

Paprika, 2 Tbsp.

Ground cumin, 1 Tbsp.

Jalapeño pepper, 1 small seeded and coarsely chopped

Extra virgin olive oil, ⅓ cup

Lemon juice, 2 Tbsp.

Wooden skewers, 12 (6-inch)

Vegetable cooking spray

Kosher salt, ½ tsp.

Drink: Italian Corvina (Ripasso)

"When I was in Thailand, I made curry paste with a huge mortar and pestle made from a hollowed-out tree trunk. It was so delicious and fun to make that I hate to admit you can buy equally tasty curry pastes at your grocer."

Kaffir lime leaves + ginger + lemon grass + red curry paste

Thai Shrimp Curry

1 Peel shrimp; devein, if desired.

2 Sauté carrots and next 2 ingredients in hot oil in a 6-qt. Dutch oven over medium-high heat 5 minutes or until onion begins to soften. Stir in lime leaves and next 2 ingredients, and cook 2 minutes or until onion is translucent.

3 Stir in curry paste, and cook 1 minute. Add broth, scraping to loosen particles from bottom of Dutch oven. Increase heat to high. Bring to a boil. Add coconut milk, and return to a boil. Reduce heat to medium low, and simmer, stirring occasionally, 15 minutes or until slightly thickened.

4 Increase heat to medium; add shrimp, and cook 4 minutes or just until shrimp turn pink. Remove and discard lime leaves. Serve over hot cooked rice, if desired. Garnish, if desired. 6 servings

Unpeeled medium-size raw shrimp, 2 lb. (16/20 count)

Carrots, 2 cups thinly sliced matchsticks

Sweet potatoes, 2 cups peeled and diced

Yellow onion, 1 small thinly sliced

Canola oil, ¼ cup

Kaffir lime leaves, 4

Fresh ginger, 2 Tbsp. peeled and grated

Fresh lemon grass, 2 Tbsp. finely chopped

Red curry paste, ¼ cup

Chicken broth, 1 (16-oz.) carton

Coconut milk, 1 (13.5-oz.) can

Hot cooked jasmine rice (optional)

Garnishes: chopped fresh cilantro, coarsely chopped peanuts, mango chutney

Drink: Belgian Witbier

coconut milk + ginger + lemon grass + basil

"Quintessential Thai flavors like chiles and coconut milk work their magic on these mussels and create a flavorful broth worth sipping."

Thai Mussels

1 Whisk together first 6 ingredients in a Dutch oven over medium heat. Bring to a boil; add mussels, and stir. Reduce heat to medium low. Cover and cook 5 minutes. Uncover, stir in basil and lime juice, and cook 1 minute or until mussel shells open. (Discard any unopened mussels.) Divide mussels between 4 individual serving bowls, and top each with about 1 cup cooking liquid. Garnish, if desired. Serve immediately. 4 servings

Coconut milk, 1 (13.5-oz.) can
Chicken broth, 1 cup
Tomatoes, 1 cup diced
Fresh ginger, ¼ cup chopped
Fresh lemon grass, 1 Tbsp. diced
Dried Thai chile peppers, 1 Tbsp. minced
Fresh mussels, 3 lb. scrubbed and debearded
Fresh basil leaves, 1 bunch (about 1 oz.)
Fresh lime juice, ¼ cup
Garnishes: fresh cilantro, lime wedges

Drink: South African Chenin Blanc/
Steen

"Chinese mustard gives this butter sauce a kick that works beautifully with mussels."

Chinese mustard + garlic + green onions + parsley

Grilled Mussel Hobo Packs with Spicy Mustard Butter

Unsalted butter, 1 cup at room temperature

Chinese mustard, 3 Tbsp.

Garlic, 2 cloves minced

Green onions, 3 finely chopped (3 Tbsp.)

Cold-water mussels, 3 lb. scrubbed and debearded

Country bread slices, 6

Olive oil, ¼ cup

Fresh flat-leaf parsley, 3 Tbsp. chopped

Drink: Provence Rosé

1 Stir together first 4 ingredients in a small bowl. Place mixture on a large piece of plastic wrap or wax paper, and shape into 2 (18-inch) logs. Freeze 1 hour or up to 1 month.

2 Preheat grill to 400° to 450° (high) heat. Stack 2 (18-inch-long) sheets of aluminum foil on top of one another. Place about 16 mussels in center of foil; top with 6 (1-inch-thick) slices frozen butter mixture. Fold both sheets of foil up, forming a packet. Repeat procedure 5 times with remaining mussels and butter.

3 Place foil packets directly on grill, seam sides up; grill, covered with grill lid, 10 minutes or until mussel shells open. (Discard any unopened mussels.)

4 Brush both sides of bread with oil. Grill bread, uncovered, 1 to 2 minutes on each side or until grill marks appear.

5 Divide mussels and any accumulated liquid among 6 individual serving bowls. Serve with grilled bread; sprinkle with parsley. 6 servings

Technique: When buying mussels, choose farm-raised and those that have been cleaned. Check for any bad ones by placing the mussels in a large bowl with a scoop of ice, a tablespoon of salt, a tablespoon of semolina, and a few cups of water. Soak for 30 minutes. Any mussels that remain open should be tossed.

"The flavors of bluefish and anchovy really work together. The sage and pancetta are a riff on Italian veal saltimbocca—a perfect pairing for this rich fish."

+

+

+

anchovy fillets   *capers*   *pancetta*   *sage leaves*

Bluefish Saltimbocca

1 Squeeze juice from 2 lemons. Cut remaining lemon into wedges.

2 Combine flour, salt, and ¼ tsp. pepper. Dredge fish in flour mixture, shaking off excess. Melt 2 Tbsp. butter with oil in a large nonstick skillet over medium-high heat. Add half of fish, and cook 3 minutes on each side or until fish flakes with a fork. Transfer fish to a serving plate, and keep warm. Repeat procedure with remaining half of fish.

3 Wipe skillet clean. Add 1 Tbsp. butter, anchovies, and next 3 ingredients, and cook over medium-high heat, stirring occasionally, 1 minute or until butter melts and garlic is tender. Add wine and lemon juice, stirring to loosen particles from bottom of skillet. Cook 3 minutes or until reduced to ⅓ cup.

4 Remove from heat, and whisk in sage and remaining 1 Tbsp. butter. Spoon sauce over fish. Sprinkle with remaining ¼ tsp. pepper. Serve with lemon wedges. 4 servings

Lemons, 3
All-purpose flour, 1½ cups
Kosher salt, ½ tsp.
Freshly ground black pepper, ½ tsp., divided
Bluefish or mackerel fillets, 8 (3- to 4-oz. each)
Butter, 4 Tbsp., divided
Vegetable oil, 2 Tbsp.
Anchovy fillets, 2 Tbsp. chopped
Capers, 4 Tbsp. drained
Garlic, 2 Tbsp. finely chopped
Pancetta, ¼ cup diced
Dry white wine, ½ cup
Fresh sage leaves, 4 chopped

"Cooking fish on the bone retains flavor and juiciness. Every home cook should know how to cook a whole fish. It is one of the simplest foods to prepare, yet it seems to be one of the most intimidating. Once you've tried it, you will see how easy it is to apply the technique to any type of whole fish."

Red snapper, 1 (4-lb.) dressed
Sea salt, 2 tsp., divided
Freshly ground black pepper, 2 tsp., divided
Lemons, 4, divided
Fresh thyme, 6 sprigs
Fresh tarragon, 6 sprigs
Extra virgin olive oil, ¼ cup
Arugula, 1½ cups
Balsamic vinegar, 2 Tbsp.

Drink: Orvieto

Baked (or Grilled) Whole Fish

1 Preheat oven to 400° (or grill to 350° to 400° for medium-high heat). Rinse fish, and pat dry. Sprinkle cavity with 1 tsp. salt and 1 tsp. pepper. Thinly slice 3 lemons. Place lemon slices, thyme, and tarragon inside cavity. Rub with oil and remaining 1 tsp. salt and 1 tsp. pepper. Place fish on a lightly greased rack in a broiler pan.

2 Bake (or grill) at 400° for 10 to 11 minutes on each side or until fish flakes with a fork.

3 Toss arugula with balsamic vinegar; place on a serving platter. Top with fish, and squeeze juice from remaining lemon over fish. 6 servings

Technique: Whole fish can certainly be served on the bone, if you'd like, for presentation; or you can remove the bone before bringing it to the table. Either way, this is the best way to do it (above).

Kids and Family

Some of my happiest memories with my children involve sitting around the table, sharing stories together while eating wonderful meals. The dinner table is one of the few places we truly connect with each other. We can turn off our phones, make eye contact, and catch up on our lives. It's the perfect way to spend time as a family. As parents, we have the opportunity to make food an important and valuable part of our children's lives. By taking a little time to cook for your children, you're giving them a gift. You're teaching them that what they put in their bodies matters, and whether they're paying attention or not, they're absorbing it. So grab your kids, get them into the kitchen, and help them become excited about food. And in 20 years, if you're lucky, they just might thank you for it!

"No other flavor combination brings me back to my childhood like this one. I still love this crunchy chicken smothered in cheese and tomato sauce.

Chicken tenders are just a clever marketing of the tenderloin of chicken breasts. It's a good thing because they cook in a mere five minutes so they're perfect weeknight fare. I'm fine using jarred sauce for this recipe, but promise me you'll look for one that isn't loaded with corn syrup or sugar. There are a ton of better options out there these days."

pasta sauce + dried oregano + mozzarella + Parmigiano-Reggiano

Chicken Tenders Parmigiano

1 Preheat oven to 350°. Pour sauce into an 11- x 7-inch baking dish.

2 Whisk together flour and next 3 ingredients. Dredge chicken in flour mixture, shaking off excess.

3 Cook chicken in 2 Tbsp. hot oil in a large sauté pan over medium-high heat 4 minutes on each side or until browned. Transfer to baking dish. Top each tender with mozzarella cheese, and sprinkle entire dish with Parmigiano-Reggiano.

4 Bake at 350° for 10 to 15 minutes or until chicken is done and cheese is bubbly. Remove from oven, and sprinkle with fresh oregano Serve over cooked spaghetti. 4 servings

Drink: Oregon Pinot Blanc or milk

Organic jarred pasta sauce, 1 cup
All-purpose flour, ½ cup
Kosher salt, ¾ tsp.
Dried oregano, ½ tsp.
Freshly ground black pepper, ½ tsp.
Chicken breast tenders, 1 lb.
Olive oil, 2 Tbsp.
Fresh mozzarella cheese, 4 oz. cut into ¼-inch-thick slices
Parmigiano-Reggiano cheese, ½ cup freshly grated
Fresh oregano, 2 tsp.
Spaghetti, 8 oz. cooked

"This recipe evolved out of a culinary 'jam session' of sorts. Amanda, my partner on this project, and I were messing around with a few kid recipes to include. She wanted to convince me that this is the way her kids love spinach. After whipping up a batch of this cheesy rice with just the right amount of spinach and crunchy cracker topping, I could see why."

Frozen spinach, 1 (16-oz.) package frozen
  leaf thawed
Yellow onion, 1 cup diced
Olive oil, 4 Tbsp.
Raisins, ½ cup
Dry mustard, ½ tsp.
Long-grain rice, 4 cups cooked
Unsalted butter, ¼ cup
All-purpose flour, ¼ cup
Kosher salt, ½ tsp.
Milk, 2 cups
Cream cheese, 1 (3-oz.) package softened
Parmigiano-Reggiano cheese, ½ cup
  shredded
Cheddar cheese, 1½ cups (6 oz.) shredded
Fish-shaped Cheddar cheese crackers,
  1½ cups
Unsalted butter, 2 Tbsp. melted

Drink: Oregon Pinot Blanc or
  lemonade

Crunchy Cheddar Cheese Casserole

❶ Preheat oven to 350°. Drain spinach well, pressing between paper towels. Chop spinach.

❷ Cook onion in hot oil in a medium-size sauté pan over medium heat, stirring often, 5 minutes or until soft. Stir in raisins, dry mustard, and spinach, and cook, stirring constantly, 2 minutes, breaking up spinach as you stir. Remove from heat, add rice, and stir until blended.

❸ Melt ¼ cup butter in a heavy saucepan over medium heat; whisk in flour and salt until smooth. Cook, whisking constantly, 1 minute. Gradually whisk in milk; cook over medium-high heat, whisking constantly, 3 minutes or until mixture is thickened and bubbly. Stir in cream cheese, and cook 2 minutes or until melted. Remove from heat, and stir in Parmigiano-Reggiano cheese until smooth.

❹ Stir together cheese sauce and spinach mixture. Let cool 1 to 3 minutes, and stir in Cheddar cheese. Pour into a lightly greased 11- x 7-inch baking dish, and spread in an even layer.

❺ Place crackers in a zip-top plastic freezer bag; seal bag, and crush crackers using a rolling pin into pea-size pieces. Pour into a bowl, and stir in 2 Tbsp. melted butter. Sprinkle cracker mixture over spinach mixture in baking dish.

❻ Bake at 350° for 35 minutes or until topping is crunchy and mixture is thoroughly heated. 8 servings

"This is a nod to my 'Southern/Italian' roots, as opposed to my 'Southern Italian' roots! The buttermilk biscuit is all Georgia, and the grated Parmigiano-Reggiano is all Italian. I've never had a better biscuit."

Parmigiano-Reggiano + buttermilk + butter

Parmesan Buttermilk Biscuits

1 Preheat oven to 400°. Combine first 7 ingredients a large bowl; cut in ½ cup chilled butter with a pastry blender or fork until crumbly. Add buttermilk, stirring with a fork just until dry ingredients are moistened.

2 Turn dough out onto a lightly floured surface. Pat or roll dough to ½-inch thickness; cut with a 2½-inch round cutter, and place 2 inches apart on a baking sheet. Brush with melted butter, and sprinkle with 1 Tbsp. Parmigiano-Reggiano cheese.

3 Bake at 400° for 15 minutes or until golden brown. 1 dozen

 **buttermilk** (BUHT-ter-milk) n. A tangy liquid that, when stirred into quick breads and cake batters, adds tenderness and flavor. "Real" buttermilk is the butter-flecked liquid left after hours of churning butter. Commercial, refrigerated versions are made thick and tart by special cultures added to milk. Buttermilk will separate and break down when heated to a near boil, so it's used mostly in baking or in cold soups, smoothies, and ice cream.

All-purpose flour, 1 cup
Cake flour, 1 cup
Parmigiano-Reggiano cheese, 1 cup freshly grated
Sugar, 1 Tbsp.
Baking powder, 1 tsp.
Baking soda, 1 tsp.
Salt, ¼ tsp.
Unsalted butter, ½ cup chilled cut into cubes
Buttermilk, 1 cup
Unsalted butter, 2 Tbsp. melted
Parmigiano-Reggiano cheese, 1 Tbsp. freshly grated

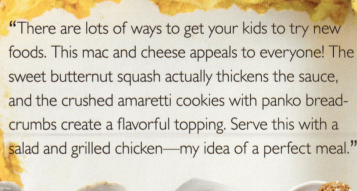

"There are lots of ways to get your kids to try new foods. This mac and cheese appeals to everyone! The sweet butternut squash actually thickens the sauce, and the crushed amaretti cookies with panko breadcrumbs create a flavorful topping. Serve this with a salad and grilled chicken—my idea of a perfect meal."

 + +

nutmeg + Parmigiano-Reggiano + ricotta + amaretti cookies

Butternut Mac 'n' Cheese

Unsalted butter, 2 Tbsp.

Butternut squash, 4 cups peeled and diced (about 1 lb.)

Penne pasta, 3½ cups (12 oz.) uncooked

Heavy cream, 2 cups

Ground nutmeg, ⅛ tsp.

Parmigiano-Reggiano cheese, ½ cup finely grated, divided

Ricotta cheese, ¼ cup

Kosher salt, 1 tsp.

Freshly ground black pepper, ¼ tsp.

Amaretti cookies, 2 crushed

Panko breadcrumbs, ½ cup

❶ Preheat oven to 350°. Melt butter in a large skillet over medium-high heat; add squash, and cook, stirring occasionally, 10 minutes or until golden brown. Add 2 cups water; cover and cook 5 minutes or until squash is tender. Drain.

❷ Prepare pasta according to package directions.

❸ Meanwhile, stir together cream, nutmeg, and ¼ cup Parmigiano-Reggiano cheese in a large saucepan. Cook over medium-low heat, stirring occasionally, 7 minutes or until mixture begins to thicken. Stir in squash. Process mixture with a handheld blender until smooth. (Or, let mixture cool 20 minutes, and process, in batches, in a food processor or blender until smooth.) Stir in ricotta, salt, and pepper.

❹ Stir together hot cooked pasta and squash mixture. Pour into a buttered 11- x 7-inch baking dish. Stir together cookies and panko, and sprinkle over pasta mixture. Top with remaining ¼ cup Parmigiano-Reggiano cheese. Cover tightly.

❺ Bake at 350° for 20 minutes. Uncover and bake 7 minutes or until top is browned. Serve immediately. 6 to 8 servings

Note: For a less sweet dish, omit the amaretti cookies and double the panko.

Drink: Horchata, a traditional Central American drink made from toasted almonds, vanilla, cinnamon, and rice. Great for kids and adults alike!

"I want you to think of this sauce as a version of fast food for your family. Loaded with fresh veggies and meat (and a little nutmeg for a surprise), this sauce is irresistible to almost everyone. You can make a double batch of it and freeze half for later. Then toss it with your favorite fettuccine or pappardelle whenever you're in a pinch, and dinner is served."

garlic + *cinnamon* + *allspice* + *nutmeg*

Bolognese

1 Brown first 3 ingredients in a large Dutch oven over medium-high heat, stirring often, 8 minutes or until meat crumbles and is no longer pink; drain, reserving 2 Tbsp. drippings in Dutch oven.

2 Add olive oil to hot drippings. Reduce heat to medium, and add garlic. Cook, stirring often, 1 minute. Add onion and next 2 ingredients, and cook, stirring often, 8 minutes or until vegetables are softened. Stir in meat, tomatoes, and next 7 ingredients.

3 Bring to a boil, reduce heat to medium low, and simmer, stirring occasionally, 1½ hours or until liquid is reduced by about one-third. Stir in cream and butter, and cook 10 minutes. Discard cinnamon sticks. 11 cups

Note: I suggest using San Marzano canned tomatoes.

bolognese **(boh-loh-NYE-ze) n.** A thick Italian sauce for pasta made from ground meat, tomatoes, celery, carrots, and sometimes bacon, and seasoned with garlic, herbs, and olive oil. Also refers to foods prepared in the cooking style of Bologna, Italy.

Ground beef, 1 lb.
Ground veal, ½ lb.
Ground pork, ½ lb.
Extra virgin olive oil, ½ cup
Garlic, 2 Tbsp. chopped
Yellow onion, ⅓ cup finely chopped
Carrots, ⅓ cup finely chopped
Celery ribs, ⅓ cup finely chopped
Diced tomatoes, 1 (28-oz.) can
Tomato puree, 1 (28-oz.) can
Chicken broth, 1½ cups
Cinnamon sticks, 2
Kosher salt, 1 tsp.
Ground allspice, ½ tsp.
Ground nutmeg, ½ tsp.
Freshly ground black pepper, ½ tsp.
Heavy cream, 1 cup
Unsalted butter, ¼ cup

Drink: Super Tuscan/Italian blend or milk

"There's a reason why pizza continues to be the #1 most consumed food in the world. It's the best of everything—doughy crust, gooey cheese, and tomatoey sauce. When it's great, it's truly great. And your kids will love coming up with their own combos. If you're in a rush, just ask your favorite pizza place for some pre-made dough that's already been out at room temp. You'll have fresh pizzas baked up in no time!"

 + +

extra virgin olive oil   *mozzarella*   *basil*   *oregano*

Classic Pizza

Tomato Sauce

Canned tomatoes, 1 (28-oz.) can drained
Extra virgin olive oil, 2 Tbsp.
Dried oregano, ½ tsp.
Kosher salt, 1 tsp.
Freshly ground black pepper, ½ tsp.

Pizza

All-purpose flour
Whole-wheat or plain pizza dough round,
  1 (2-lb.) bakery or homemade (page 34)

Toppings

Fresh mozzarella cheese, 4 oz. torn into
  small pieces
Fresh basil leaves

Drink: California Syrah or
  Italian soda

❶ Preheat oven to 450°. If using a pizza stone, place in oven to preheat.

❷ To prepare tomato sauce, place tomatoes in a large bowl, and crush to desired consistency using your hands. (Or, process tomatoes in a food processor until pureed.) Stir in olive oil, oregano, salt, and pepper.

❸ To prepare pizza, sprinkle flour on a large, flat surface. Divide dough into 4 (8-oz.) rounds. Roll each round into a 12-inch diameter, sprinkling surface with flour as needed to prevent sticking. Transfer to a lightly greased baking sheet or preheated pizza stone.

❹ Spread ½ cup sauce over dough, leaving a ½-inch border. (Reserve remaining sauce for another use.) Top with cheese.

5 Bake at 450° on bottom oven rack 10 minutes or until cheese is melted and crust is golden. Remove from oven, and top with basil. *4 pizzas (4 to 6 servings)*

Note: I suggest using San Marzano canned tomatoes.

Pesto Pizza: Omit tomato sauce and basil. Prepare recipe as directed, spreading 2 Tbsp. My Favorite Pesto (page 28) over crust and topping pizza with 2 Tbsp. pine nuts (in addition to mozzarella cheese) in Step 4. Top with 2 cups arugula after baking.

Salami-and-Caramelized Onion Pizza: Omit basil. Cook 1 large sweet onion, halved and thinly sliced, in 2 Tbsp. hot olive oil in a large skillet over medium heat, stirring occasionally, 10 minutes or until light golden. Stir in 1 tsp. sugar, ½ tsp. kosher salt, and ⅛ tsp. freshly ground black pepper. Cook, stirring often, 8 minutes or until onions are caramel colored. Stir in 1 Tbsp. balsamic vinegar, and cook 2 minutes. Prepare recipe as directed, spreading caramelized onions over tomato sauce and topping pizza with 2 oz. thinly sliced salami (in addition to mozzarella cheese) in Step 4.

Salad Pizza: Omit tomato sauce, mozzarella cheese, and basil. Prepare recipe as directed, brushing 2 tsp. olive oil over dough before topping with mozzarella. Toss together 3 cups arugula, 1 cup diced heirloom or cherry tomatoes, 1 Tbsp. olive oil, 1 Tbsp. fresh lemon juice, and ¼ tsp. kosher salt in a large bowl. Top hot, baked pizza with arugula mixture and ⅓ cup shaved Parmigiano-Reggiano cheese.

"Loaded with aromatics, this marinade is a perfect match for grilled steaks. Marinate the steak for a few hours to really soak up the flavors, and serve it thinly sliced with my Parsnip Puree (page 113) or Parmigiano-Reggiano Potato Wedges (facing page). We used the marinade with the sliced beef tenderloin on our cover."

Soy sauce, 1 cup
Balsamic vinegar, ½ cup
Brown sugar, ¼ cup firmly packed
Worcestershire sauce, ¼ cup
Sesame oil, ¼ cup
Fresh ginger, 3 Tbsp. chopped
Sriracha sauce, 1 Tbsp.*
Garlic, 3 cloves chopped
Skirt steak, 3 lb.
Kosher salt and freshly
   ground black pepper
   to taste

soy sauce   +   brown sugar   +   sesame oil   +   ginger

Ginger-Soy Skirt Steak

1 Whisk together first 8 ingredients and 1 cup water in a large shallow dish or zip-top plastic freezer bag; add steak. Cover or seal, and chill 2 to 6 hours.

2 Preheat grill to 350° to 400° (medium-high) heat. Remove steak from marinade, discarding marinade. Let stand at room temperature 15 minutes. Sprinkle with desired amount of salt and pepper.

3 Grill steak, covered with grill lid, 8 minutes or to desired degree of doneness. Let stand 10 minutes. Cut steak diagonally across the grain into thin slices. 6 to 8 servings

*Substitute 1 chopped jalapeño pepper for sriracha sauce.

Drink: Dark and Stormier (page 47)

"French fries are my weak spot. So if your kids are already hooked like I am, you'll love this baked version that is a lot better for them. If you want to make a party out of it, serve a pile of these fries with all my favorite condiments: my Spiced Ketchup (page 24), a few Aiolis (page 22), and plain ketchup for the kiddos, of course. You can always experiment with different types of potatoes, too. The sky is the limit!"

olive oil + Parmigiano-Reggiano + parsley

Parmigiano-Reggiano Potato Wedges

1 Preheat oven to 450°. Place 2 baking sheets in oven to heat.

2 Cut potatoes into ½-inch-thick wedges. Place potatoes and 2 qt. cold water in a large bowl, and let stand 2 minutes; drain. Repeat procedure, if necessary, until water is no longer cloudy. Pat potatoes completely dry. (Soggy potatoes will result in soggy fries.) Toss potatoes in oil, and arrange in a single layer on 2 hot baking sheets.

3 Bake at 450° for 20 to 25 minutes or until skin is crispy and potatoes are tender, stirring halfway through. Remove from oven, and sprinkle with Parmigiano-Reggiano cheese, salt, and pepper. Top with parsley just before serving, if desired. 4 servings

Baking potatoes, 2
Cold water, 2 qt.
Olive oil, 1 Tbsp.
Parmigiano-Reggiano cheese, ½ cup freshly grated
Kosher salt, ¾ tsp.
Freshly ground black pepper, ¼ tsp.
Fresh flat-leaf parsley, 2 Tbsp. chopped (optional)

"This meal is totally meant for spring, when salmon is at its best, peas are ripe from the garden, and parsnips planted in the fall are being pulled from the ground. The elements on the plate provide an equal dose of eye candy and taste bud treat. This a great way to get finicky kids to eat their vegetables."

olive oil + *salt* + *pepper*

Pan-Seared Salmon with Parsnip Puree

Salmon fillets, 4 (6-oz.) skin-on
Olive oil, 7 tsp., divided
Kosher salt, ¼ tsp.
Freshly ground black pepper, ¼ tsp.
Parsnip Puree (page 113)
Fresh Pea Medley (page 215, optional)

Drink: Washington Pinot Noir

❶ Preheat oven to 400°. Rinse fish, and pat dry with a paper towel. Rub 1 tsp. olive oil over each fillet, and season with salt and pepper.

❷ Cook fish, skin sides up, in remaining 1 Tbsp. hot oil in a large ovenproof sauté pan over medium-high heat 2 to 3 minutes; flip fish, and cook 2 minutes.

❸ Bake at 400° for 3 to 6 minutes or to desired degree of doneness.

❹ Spoon Parsnip Puree into 4 individual serving bowls. Top each with 1 fillet. Serve with Fresh Pea Medley, if desired. 4 servings

sear (SEER) v. Browning meat quickly on all sides over high heat in a skillet, under a broiler, or in a very hot oven. Searing is usually done to give it a richer, more complex flavor before it's braised. Searing is claimed to seal in the meat's juices.

Fresh Pea Medley

1 Cook snow and sugar snap peas in hot oil in a large sauté pan over medium-high heat, stirring constantly, 2 to 4 minutes or until crisp-tender. Add sweet peas, and cook, stirring often, 1 minute or until thoroughly heated. Remove from heat.

2 Squeeze juice from lemon half. Stir lemon juice, salt, and pepper into pea mixture. 7 servings

Variation: Add 1 cup fresh pea shoots at end of Step 1. Stir in 1 cup crabmeat with lemon juice.

*Substitute frozen sweet peas if you can't find fresh.

Fresh snow peas, 1 cup
Fresh sugar snap peas, 1 cup
Olive oil, 1 Tbsp.
Fresh sweet peas, 1 cup*
Lemon, ½
Kosher salt, ½ tsp.
Freshly ground black pepper, ¼ tsp.

"Everyone should know how to make double-stuffed potatoes, because it seems like everyone from age 1 to 100 will eat them! These are great as an entrée with a salad or served alongside one of my T-bones (page 168) for an over-the-top, restaurant-quality dinner. 'Papas' is the Spanish word for potatoes, and I just like saying it because that's how most dads will feel after eating these."

butter   +   sour cream   +   chives

Double-Stuffed Papas

Baking potatoes, 4
Unsalted butter, ¼ cup
Sour cream, ½ cup
Milk, ½ cup
Kosher salt, 1 tsp.
Freshly ground black pepper, ½ tsp.
Fresh chives, 3 Tbsp. finely chopped,
    divided

❶ Preheat oven to 375°. Bake potatoes at 375° on a baking sheet 1 hour or until tender. Let potatoes cool 10 minutes.

❷ Meanwhile, melt butter in a heavy saucepan over medium-low heat, stirring constantly, 8 minutes or just until butter begins to turn golden brown. Immediately remove from heat, and pour butter into a small bowl. (Butter will continue to darken if left in pan.)

❸ Cut potatoes in half lengthwise. Carefully scoop out potato pulp into a bowl, leaving shells intact. Add sour cream, milk, and browned butter to potato pulp in bowl, and mash until blended and desired consistency. Stir in salt, pepper, and 2 Tbsp. chives. Spoon mixture into each potato shell, and place on baking sheet.

❹ Bake at 375° for 15 minutes or until tops are browned. Sprinkle with remaining 1 Tbsp. chives just before serving. 8 servings

milk + egg + yogurt + syrup

Pigs in a Pancake

1 Whisk together first 4 ingredients in a large bowl just until blended. (Batter will be thick.)

2 Thread 1 sausage lengthwise onto each skewer, leaving 4 to 5 inches of skewer on one side as a handle.

3 Pour oil to a depth of 3 inches into a Dutch oven; heat over medium heat to 365°. Dip skewers in pancake batter, shaking off excess. Fry skewers, in batches, 2 minutes or until golden brown, turning often. (Use metal tongs to keep skewers submerged while frying.) Drain on a wire rack over paper towels.

4 Stir together yogurt and syrup in a bowl. Serve skewers with yogurt mixture and, if desired, Spiced Apple Compote. 4 servings

Drink: Mimosas or milk

"This is a new spin on Pigs in a Blanket, and it's even more fun skewered. Breakfast sausage gets coated in pancake batter, then deep fried. Dunked in maple yogurt or served with my Spiced Apple Compote (page 228), this is the ultimate family breakfast. Don't come looking for me when you're addicted."

Just-add-water pancake-and-waffle mix, 1 cup
Milk, ⅔ cup
Large egg, 1
Vegetable oil, 1 Tbsp.
Precooked breakfast sausage links, 8
Wooden skewers, 8 (8-inch)
Vegetable oil
Low-fat plain yogurt, 1 cup
Pure maple syrup, 2 Tbsp.
Spiced Apple Compote (page 228) or
  applesauce (optional)

Desserts

Desserts don't need to be an everyday occurrence, but they are a wonderful way to round out a great meal. When making desserts, I don't believe in trying to reduce calories or create low-fat versions so we can eat more of something. I'd much rather have full-flavored, knock-your-socks-off desserts that will send you away with the perfect taste in your mouth—literally! And with a great dessert, you need only a couple of bites to satiate a sweet tooth. Make your way through this chapter loaded with my all-time favorites, and you will have mastered the most important techniques in dessert making, from cooking crème anglaise for ice cream to making homemade caramel. So come on, live a little and stay for dessert!

"The clean, bright flavors of one of my favorite summer cocktails becomes a perfectly refreshing dessert for slurping."

Superfine sugar, ½ cup
Light rum, 5 Tbsp.
Fresh lime juice, ¼ cup
Fresh mint sprigs, 3 large coarsely chopped

sugar + *rum* + *lime juice* + *mint*

Mojito Pops

1 Stir together first 3 ingredients and 2 cups water in a bowl, stirring until sugar is dissolved. Stir in mint.

2 Pour mixture into 8 (3-oz.) plastic pop molds. Top with lids of pop molds, and insert craft sticks, leaving 1½ to 2 inches of each sticking out. Freeze 4 hours or until sticks are solidly anchored and pops are completely frozen. 8 servings

"Pound cake is a classic, but the olive oil gives this cake a certain crumb that is totally modern. Served with a scoop of my Vanilla Ice Cream (page 226) with a pile of fresh berries on top, or toasted for breakfast, this is killer."

lemon zest   +   orange zest   +   vanilla bean   +   olive oil

Olive Oil Pound Cake

1 Preheat oven to 350°. Coat a 9- x 5-inch pan with cooking spray. Line bottom of pan with parchment paper, and coat paper with cooking spray. Dust bottom of pan with 2 tsp. flour.

2 Beat together sugar and next 3 ingredients at medium speed with a heavy-duty electric stand mixer until well blended (about 5 minutes). Add eggs, 1 at a time, beating until blended after each addition. Beat in vanilla bean paste, scraping bottom and sides of bowl as needed.

3 Whisk together 1¾ cups flour and next 3 ingredients. Stir together olive oil and buttermilk. Add flour mixture to sugar mixture alternately with olive oil mixture, beginning and ending with flour mixture. Beat well after each addition until blended. Pour batter into prepared pan.

4 Bake at 350° for 45 to 50 minutes or until a wooden pick inserted in center comes out clean. Let cool on a wire rack 10 minutes. Remove from pan to wire rack, and let cool completely (about 1 hour). 8 servings

Vegetable cooking spray
Parchment paper
All-purpose flour, 2 tsp.
Sugar, 1 cup
Unsalted butter, ¼ cup softened
Lemon zest, 2 tsp.
Orange zest, 2 tsp.
Large eggs, 3
Vanilla bean paste, 1 Tbsp.
All-purpose flour, 1¾ cups
Baking powder, 1½ tsp.
Kosher salt, ½ tsp.
Baking soda, ¼ tsp.
Olive oil, 1 cup
Buttermilk, ½ cup

"We all know The King of Rock-n-Roll had a peanut butter and banana obsession, but this recipe takes it one step further. If you really want to make him proud, my grape marshmallows make this insane!"

Creamy peanut butter, 6 Tbsp.
Bananas, 2 ripe finely chopped
Bittersweet chocolate baking bar, 4 oz. chopped
Milk, 2 cups
Grape Marshmallows*

Grape juice, ⅓ cup plus 1 Tbsp.
Unflavored gelatin, 4 tsp.
Powdered sugar, 1 cup
Cornstarch, 1 cup
Granulated sugar, 1 cup plus 1 Tbsp.
Light corn syrup, 1 Tbsp.
Large egg white, 1

peanut butter + bananas + bittersweet chocolate + milk

Elvis Hot Chocolate

❶ Place first 3 ingredients in a ovenproof bowl.

❷ Cook milk in a nonaluminum saucepan over medium heat 4 minutes or until almost boiling. Pour over ingredients in bowl. Let stand 1 minute. Process mixture using a hand-held blender until smooth. Cook over low heat 2 minutes or until thoroughly heated. Pour into 4 (8-oz.) mugs, and top with marshmallows. Serve immediately. 4 servings

*Miniature marshmallows may be substituted.

grape marshmallows:

❶ Combine grape juice and gelatin in a bowl; let stand.

❷ Stir together powdered sugar and cornstarch in a bowl. Sprinkle half of mixture in an even layer in a 9-inch square cake pan.

❸ Cook granulated sugar, corn syrup, and ⅓ cup water in a saucepan over medium-high heat, without stirring, 8 minutes or until a candy thermometer registers 121°.

❹ Meanwhile, beat egg white at medium speed with a heavy-duty electric stand mixture, using whisk attachment, until frothy. Add sugar–corn syrup mixture to egg white, beating until blended. Beat in gelatin mixture. Beat at high speed 10 minutes or until thickened.

❺ Pour mixture into prepared pan. Sprinkle with remaining half of powdered sugar–cornstarch mixture. Chill 15 minutes. Cut into squares. 36 (1½-inch) marshmallows

"My favorite cookie has everything in it but the kitchen sink! I love the variation of chips, but use this recipe as a base and add whatever type of chips you like. Nuts are purely optional, but I love the crunch in contrast to all those gooey, melted chips."

 + +

Chocolate morsels   *peanut butter morsels*   *walnuts*

Todd's Favorite Cookies

1 Preheat oven to 350°. Beat butter, granulated sugar, and brown sugar at medium speed with an electric mixer until smooth. Add eggs, 1 at a time, beating until blended after each addition. Stir in vanilla.

2 Combine flour and next 3 ingredients. Gradually add to butter mixture, and beat until blended after each addition. Stir in semisweet chocolate, next 3 ingredients, and, if desired, peanut butter morsels. Drop by 2 tablespoonfuls onto ungreased baking sheets.

3 Bake at 350° for 10 to 12 minutes or until edges are browned. Cool on baking sheets 2 minutes. Remove from baking sheets to a wire rack. 4 dozen

Unsalted butter, 1 cup softened
Granulated sugar, 1 cup
Firmly packed brown sugar, 1 cup
Large eggs, 2
Vanilla extract, 2 tsp.
All-purpose flour, 3 cups
Baking soda, 1 tsp.
Kosher salt, 1 tsp.
Baking powder, ¼ tsp.
Semisweet chocolate morsels, 1½ cups
Milk chocolate morsels, ½ cup
White chocolate morsels, ½ cup
Walnuts, ½ cup coarsely chopped
Peanut butter morsels, ¼ cup
 (optional)

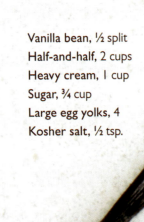

"A total classic! Once you learn how to make the base for this ice cream (also known as crème anglaise in its unfrozen state), you can do all kinds of things with it in addition to the variations below. Mix in chocolate chips or fresh fruit at the end of freezing, or serve it with chopped bananas and chocolate and caramel sauce for a sundae. Or smother it in Spiced Apple Compote (page 228) for the perfect end to a dinner party."

vanilla bean   +   cream   +   sugar

Vanilla Ice Cream

Vanilla bean, ½ split
Half-and-half, 2 cups
Heavy cream, 1 cup
Sugar, ¾ cup
Large egg yolks, 4
Kosher salt, ½ tsp.

1 Scrape seeds from vanilla bean; chop bean.

2 Bring chopped vanilla bean and seeds, half-and-half, and next 2 ingredients to a boil in a medium saucepan over medium-high heat. Remove from heat, transfer to a bowl, and let stand 30 minutes.

3 Stir together egg yolks and salt in a large bowl.

4 Return vanilla bean mixture to saucepan, and bring to a boil over medium-high heat. Remove from heat. Gradually stir about one-fourth of hot vanilla mixture into yolks; add yolk mixture to remaining hot vanilla mixture, stirring constantly.

5 Cook over low heat, stirring constantly, 3 minutes or until mixture coats the back of a spoon. Pour through a fine wire-mesh strainer into a bowl; discard solids.

6 Fill a large bowl with ice. Place bowl containing vanilla mixture in ice, and let stand, stirring occasionally, until completely cool (about 3 hours).

7 Pour mixture into freezer container of a 2-qt. electric ice-cream maker, and freeze according to manufacturer's instructions. (Instructions and times may vary.) 1½ qt.

Strawberry Ice Cream: Stir together 2½ cups chopped fresh strawberries and ¼ cup sugar; let stand 1 hour. Prepare recipe as directed. Before transferring ice cream to a container for further freezing, stir in strawberry mixture.

Peppermint Ice Cream: Chop ½ cup loosely packed fresh peppermint leaves. Bring peppermint leaves to a boil with vanilla bean in Step 2. Proceed with recipe as directed through Step 4. Stir in ¼ tsp. peppermint extract. Proceed as directed in Steps 5 through 7. Before transferring ice cream to a container for further freezing, stir in 20 crushed peppermint candies.

"Apples are so good on their own, and I love that this compote highlights their flavor. Use an assortment of apples suited for baking, such as Gala, Granny Smith, and McIntosh."

vanilla bean + butter + cinnamon (stick & ground) + raisins

Spiced Apple Compote

① Scrape seeds from vanilla bean. Bring vanilla bean and seeds, sugar, and next 6 ingredients to a simmer in a stockpot or large sauce pan over high heat. Add apples and raisins, and bring to a boil. Reduce heat to medium-low, and simmer, stirring often, 40 minutes or until mixture thickens and apples soften and begin to break down.

② Remove from heat. Stir in apple brandy. Serve immediately with ice cream.
12 cups

Note: Let mixture cool completely (about 2 hours) before chilling any leftovers. Remove cinnamon sticks and vanilla bean before reheating.

Vanilla bean, 1 split
Sugar, 2½ cups
Unsalted butter, 2 cups
Cinnamon sticks, 2
Kosher salt, 1 Tbsp.
Ground cinnamon, 2 tsp.
Ground ginger, 1 tsp.
Ground nutmeg, 1 tsp.
Assorted apples, 14 large peeled and
    quartered
Raisins, ½ cup
Apple brandy (Calvados), ¼ cup
Vanilla Ice Cream (page 226)

"This is so much better than what you can buy in a jar. Serve this over my Vanilla Ice Cream (page 226) or Peppermint Ice Cream (page 227), or just eat it with a spoon out of the fridge like I do."

sugar + cocoa + peanut butter + vanilla extract

Peanut Butter Hot Fudge

1 Melt butter and chocolate in a small, nonaluminum saucepan over medium-low heat. Stir in sugar and cocoa until blended. Gradually add evaporated milk, stirring until blended.

2 Bring to a low simmer over medium heat, stirring constantly. Remove from heat when bubbles appear. Stir in peanut butter and remaining ingredients. Serve warm. 2 cups

Unsalted butter, ½ cup
Unsweetened chocolate baking bar, 1 oz.
Sugar, ¾ cup
Unsweetened cocoa, ¼ cup
Evaporated milk, 1 (5-oz.) can
Creamy peanut butter, ½ cup
Vanilla extract, 1 tsp.
Kosher salt, ¼ tsp.

"I'm constantly driving my team crazy by 'Todd-izing' classic recipes. But I love finding one unique twist on classics. Soy milk has never tasted as good as it does in this version of Panna Cotta. The creamy texture of the soy milk is perfect with the bright, clean flavor of the blackberries."

vanilla bean + soy milk + sugar + blackberries

Vanilla bean, 1 split
Unflavored gelatin, 1 Tbsp.
Unsweetened soy milk, 2 cups
Sugar, ½ cup
Kosher salt, 1 tsp., divided
Plain soy yogurt, 2 cups
Fresh blackberries, 1 pt.
Sugar, 2 Tbsp.
Garnish: crushed amaretti cookies

Soy Milk Panna Cotta with Crushed Blackberries

❶ Scrape seeds from vanilla bean.

❷ Stir together gelatin and ¼ cup water in a small bowl.

❸ Bring milk, ½ cup sugar, ¾ tsp. salt, and vanilla bean and seeds to a simmer in a medium saucepan over medium-high heat; reduce heat to medium. Whisk in gelatin mixture until well blended.

❹ Bring to a simmer, stirring constantly, and cook 1 minute. Remove from heat, and discard vanilla bean. Stir in yogurt until blended. Pour mixture through a fine wire-mesh strainer into a bowl; discard solids.

❺ Divide mixture among 6 (6-oz.) ramekins. Cover and chill 3 hours or until set.

❻ Stir together blackberries, 2 Tbsp. sugar, and remaining ¼ tsp. salt in a bowl. Gently crush blackberries against sides of bowl until berries release their juices, using a fork. Let stand 10 minutes.

❼ Cook berry mixture in a small skillet over medium-high heat, stirring occasionally, 3 minutes or until liquid begins to thicken. Let cool 5 minutes.

❽ Hold each ramekin in warm water 5 seconds; invert onto serving plates. Top with blackberry sauce. Garnish, if desired. 6 servings

"Learning how to make caramel is crucial in a pastry kitchen. Using my recipe, you can learn to make it at home and you will use it all the time. This combination is unlike any crispy rice treat you've ever tasted!"

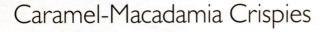

butter   +   crisp rice cereal   +   macadamia nuts   +   semisweet chocolate morsels

Caramel-Macadamia Crispies

❶ Line a 13- x 9-inch pan with parchment paper; coat with cooking spray.

❷ Cook sugar and 6 Tbsp. water in a large sauté pan over high heat, whisking constantly, 5 to 9 minutes or until sugar caramelizes. Carefully and slowly stir in cream and butter, whisking constantly. Remove from heat, and stir in vanilla and salt.

❸ Stir together cereal and nuts in a large bowl. Pour caramel over cereal mixture, and stir until well blended, using a wooden spoon. Spread mixture in an even layer in prepared pan (about ½ to 1 inch thick), using a plastic spatula or lightly buttered hands. Cover and chill 10 to 20 minutes or until firm.

❹ Microwave chocolate in a glass measuring cup at HIGH 1 minute or until melted and smooth, stirring at 30-second intervals. Invert cereal mixture onto a cutting board; cut into 24 squares. Drizzle with melted chocolate, and sprinkle each with a tiny pinch of sea salt. 2 dozen

Parchment paper
Vegetable cooking spray
Sugar, 1⅓ cups
Heavy cream, ½ cup
Unsalted butter, 2 Tbsp.
Vanilla extract, 1 Tbsp.
Kosher salt, ¾ tsp.
Crisp rice cereal, 4 cups
Macadamia nuts, 1 cup chopped
Semisweet chocolate morsels, ⅔ cup
Coarse sea salt

Desserts   231

"My daughter Izzy and I opened a cupcake shop in Boston. She designed the shop, the logo... everything. I can't believe her talents at 17. This has quickly become her best seller."

cocoa + sugar + sour cream + red wine vinegar

Izzy's Red Velvet Curly Cakes

Paper baking cups, 30
All-purpose flour, 2½ cups
Unsweetened cocoa, ¼ cup
Baking soda, 1 tsp.
Kosher salt, ½ tsp.
Sugar, 2 cups
Unsalted butter, 1 cup softened
Large eggs, 4
Sour cream, 1 cup
Buttermilk, ½ cup
Red wine vinegar, 2 Tbsp.
Red food coloring, 2 Tbsp.
Vanilla extract, 2 tsp.
Vanilla–Cream Cheese Frosting
White chocolate baking bars, 3 (4 oz. each)

❶ Preheat oven to 350°. Place paper baking cups in 3 (12-cup) muffin pans. Whisk together flour and next 3 ingredients in a medium bowl.

❷ Beat sugar and butter at medium speed with an electric mixer 5 minutes or until light and fluffy. Add eggs, 1 at a time, beating until blended after each addition. Beat in sour cream and next 4 ingredients just until blended. Gradually add flour mixture, beating at low speed just until blended, stopping to scrape bowl as needed. (Do not overbeat.) Spoon batter into prepared muffin cups, filling two-thirds full.

❸ Bake at 350° for 20 to 22 minutes or until a wooden pick inserted in centers comes out clean. Cool in pans on wire racks 5 minutes. Remove from pans to wire racks, and cool completely (about 45 minutes).

4 Spoon Vanilla–Cream Cheese Frosting into a zip-top plastic freezer bag (do not seal). Snip 1 corner of bag to make a small hole. Pipe frosting onto cupcakes.

5 Chill cupcakes 30 minutes or until frosting is firm.

6 Microwave white chocolate in a microwave-safe bowl at HIGH 1 minute or until melted and smooth, stirring at 30-second intervals. Gently dip tops of cupcakes into melted white chocolate. Serve at room temperature. 30 cupcakes

vanilla–cream cheese frosting:

Cream cheese, 1 (8-oz.) package softened

Cream cheese, 1 (3-oz.) package softened

Unsalted butter, 6 Tbsp. softened

Vanilla extract, 3 tsp.

Powdered sugar, 1½ (16-oz.) packages (5½ cups)

1 Beat together first 4 ingredients at medium speed with an electric mixer until light and fluffy. Gradually beat in powdered sugar just until smooth. 4 cups

"If you like chocolate like I like chocolate, then get baking! This recipe is nothing short of spectacular. It combines all the chewy, sweet things I like to combine with chocolate. And if you really want to overdo it, add the frosting!"

Brownie Hash

Unsalted butter, 1 cup
Semisweet chocolate baking bar, 1 oz.
Large eggs, 4
Sugar, 2 cups
All-purpose flour, 2 cups
Unsweetened cocoa, ½ cup
Kosher salt, 1 tsp.
Vanilla extract, 1 tsp.
Semisweet chocolate morsels, 1½ cups
Walnuts, 1½ cups chopped
Miniature marshmallows, 2 cups
Chocolate Frosting (optional)

❶ Preheat oven to 350°. Microwave butter and chocolate baking bar in a microwave-safe bowl at HIGH 2 minutes or until melted, stirring at 1-minute intervals.

❷ Beat eggs at medium speed with an electric mixer until thickened; gradually add sugar, and beat well until very thick. (Mixture will be stiff enough to fall in ribbons when beaters are lifted.) Reduce speed to low, and add flour and next 3 ingredients; beat well, scraping sides and bottom of bowl as needed.

❸ Stir in butter-chocolate mixture, morsels, and walnuts. Pour batter into a lightly greased 13- x 9-inch pan.

❹ Bake at 350° for 20 to 25 minutes or until a wooden pick inserted in center comes out clean. Sprinkle with marshmallows, and bake 3 minutes or until marshmallows are partially melted. Remove from oven to a wire rack, and let cool 5 minutes.

❺ Spread top of brownies with Chocolate Frosting, if desired. Let stand 30 minutes to 1 hour. Cut into squares. 2 dozen

chocolate frosting:

Unsalted butter, ½ cup softened
Powdered sugar, 1 (16-oz.) package
Unsweetened cocoa, 3 Tbsp.

Milk, ⅓ cup
Vanilla extract, 2 tsp.

❶ Beat butter at medium speed with an electric mixer until creamy. Add sugar and cocoa, and beat until blended. Beat in milk and vanilla until smooth. 2½ cups

Metric Equivalents

The recipes that appear in this cookbook use the standard U.S. method for measuring liquid and dry or solid ingredients (teaspoons, tablespoons, and cups). The information in the following charts is provided to help cooks outside the United States successfully use these recipes. All equivalents are approximate.

Metric Equivalents for Different Types of Ingredients

A standard cup measure of a dry or solid ingredient will vary in weight depending on the type of ingredient. A standard cup of liquid is the same volume for any type of liquid. Use the following chart when converting standard cup measures to grams (weight) or milliliters (volume).

Standard Cup	Fine Powder (ex. flour)	Grain (ex. rice)	Granular (ex. sugar)	Liquid Solids (ex. butter)	Liquid (ex. milk)
1	140 g	150 g	190 g	200 g	240 ml
¾	105 g	113 g	143 g	150 g	180 ml
⅔	93 g	100 g	125 g	133 g	160 ml
½	70 g	75 g	95 g	100 g	120 ml
⅓	47 g	50 g	63 g	67 g	80 ml
¼	35 g	38 g	48 g	50 g	60 ml
⅛	18 g	19 g	24 g	25 g	30 ml

Useful Equivalents for Liquid Ingredients by Volume

¼ tsp					=	1 ml
½ tsp					=	2 ml
1 tsp					=	5 ml
3 tsp	=	1 Tbsp	=	½ fl oz	=	15 ml
		2 Tbsp	= ⅛ cup	= 1 fl oz	=	30 ml
		4 Tbsp	= ¼ cup	= 2 fl oz	=	60 ml
		5⅓ Tbsp	= ⅓ cup	= 3 fl oz	=	80 ml
		8 Tbsp	= ½ cup	= 4 fl oz	=	120 ml
		10⅔ Tbsp	= ⅔ cup	= 5 fl oz	=	160 ml
		12 Tbsp	= ¾ cup	= 6 fl oz	=	180 ml
		16 Tbsp	= 1 cup	= 8 fl oz	=	240 ml
		1 pt	= 2 cups	= 16 fl oz	=	480 ml
		1 qt	= 4 cups	= 32 fl oz	=	960 ml
				33 fl oz	=	1000 ml = 1 l

Useful Equivalents for Dry Ingredients by Weight

(To convert ounces to grams, multiply the number of ounces by 30.)

1 oz	=	¹⁄₁₆ lb	=	30 g
4 oz	=	¼ lb	=	120 g
8 oz	=	½ lb	=	240 g
12 oz	=	¾ lb	=	360 g
16 oz	=	1 lb	=	480 g

Useful Equivalents for Length

(To convert inches to centimeters, multiply the number of inches by 2.5.)

1 in			=	2.5 cm	
6 in	= ½ ft		=	15 cm	
12 in	= 1 ft		=	30 cm	
36 in	= 3 ft	= 1 yd	=	90 cm	
40 in			=	100 cm	= 1 m

Useful Equivalents for Cooking/Oven Temperatures

	Fahrenheit	Celsius	Gas Mark
Freeze water	32° F	0° C	
Room temperature	68° F	20° C	
Boil water	212° F	100° C	
Bake	325° F	160° C	3
	350° F	180° C	4
	375° F	190° C	5
	400° F	200° C	6
	425° F	220° C	7
	450° F	230° C	8
Broil			Grill

Acknowledgments

My fourth cookbook has been a long time in the making, and I'm so proud and thrilled to finally share it with you! Working on a project like this is a truly collaborative effort, and I couldn't have done it without the hard work and creativity of so many wonderful people. I had an absolute blast working on this, so I want to take this opportunity to thank my amazing team:

Katherine Cobbs, my editor, who helped me organize all my ideas and shape my vision into a beautiful book.

Amanda Haas, my writer, who worked diligently from San Francisco at all hours of the day and night to make this book perfect! She was an enormous support, and I never could have done it with without her.

Jason Wallis, our photographer, who flew to NY and took thousands of amazing photos that really make these recipes come to life and show the true beauty and joy of what cooking is all about.

Everyone at Oxmoor House for allowing us to create this fantastic cookbook and for working so hard to ensure its success.

Bruce Lubin, my friend from Castle Point, who made this cookbook possible.

Gina Gargano, my executive assistant, who is my right hand and my left hand, and without whom nothing would get done.

Jeffrey Steelman, Katherine See, and Alfred Stephens, my corporate chefs, who tirelessly perfected the many recipes in this book, and *Doug Draper,* my wine director, who made sure the cocktails were as good as the food.

My many trusted and talented restaurant chefs, past and present, who work alongside me and whom I'm proud to have helm my kitchens.

Lindsey Valdez, who managed the countless details of this project and made sure I stayed on track.

My executive staff and management teams, who allow me to rest assured that while I am in the kitchen, my business and front of house are always running smoothly.

My many culinary mentors and colleagues, who continue to teach and inspire me every day.

And of course, my loving family: my mother, Patrizia Arunci; my oldest son, Oliver; my daughter, Isabelle; my youngest, Simon; and my niece, Tori.

Index

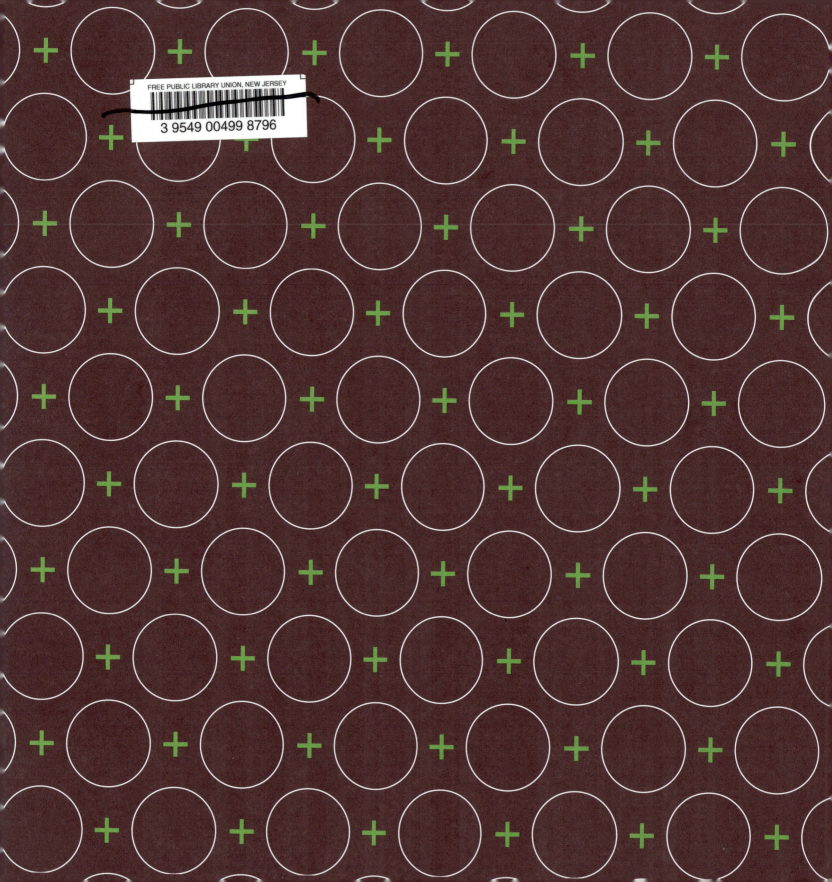